HEALING MINDFULLY

HEALING MINDFULLY

Finding peace through pain, illness, and aging

ERIN EASTON

New Leaf Mindfulness Coaching

Contents

4
MY PERSONAL HEALING JOURNEY

Preface

This topic is near and dear to my heart. Not only because of my own extensive experience with pain and illness but also because of all of my clients' experiences, my loved ones, friends, and family. Pain and illness come to all of us at some point in our lives, and being able to navigate it peacefully while staying true to our own wisdom helps us to heal to our greatest potential. I have taken many different roads to healing my aches and pains. Some were painful psychologically, emotionally, and physically while others were more harmonious. These experiences taught me how important it is to know yourself and your needs and be confident and centered enough to know how to pursue a healing journey that aligns. I hope this book helps you find a healing journey that speaks to your inner wisdom and aligns with your being, making the experience more peaceful and beneficial.

Several of the teachings in this book align with the teaching in the "Mindful of the Body" section of my book, *Living from the Heart*, and several of the exercises have been modified from that book. After writing that book, I went through anterior cruciate ligament (ACL) reconstruction surgery and spine surgery and watched several of my loved ones navigate similar surgeries, Covid, cancer, autoimmune diseases, and an array of other life-altering illnesses, which made me realize that this is a much deeper topic than I covered in the one section of that book. This book is meant to take a deeper dive into the process of healing the body, teaching you how to do so mindfully so that your illness or injury doesn't take away your peace, purpose, and happiness.

Healing the body requires acknowledging the inseparable connection of the body with the mind and the spirit. We cannot heal one without healing the others. We must address the imbalances in all of these areas to truly heal one of them. Many people have created their own interpretations of what this means with varying concentrations on one or the other. Some say that all of our physical manifestations can be altered with just the mind, others that if our spiritual connection is strong enough, we can heal all three. In my own personal experience and in my experience with my clients, I have found that all three need to be addressed equally and in balance. When we move too far to one extreme we cut off the flow between the whole system by denying the importance of the other parts.

There are so many means of healing, and this is not a one size-fits-all journey. Just because one person found success with one modality does not mean that you will find the same success. You are a different being with a different balance within you that needs different components to bring you back into homeostasis. We can learn from others and pick up what feels right to us without compromising our own truth. This is difficult in a world where everyone feels like they have the one right answer and that if everyone did the same thing, we would all be healed.

There is no ultimate healing reality. We all have the responsibility to identify and pursue our personal healing journey.

Mindfulness helps us to create this personal healing journey by building an awareness of our whole being, mind, body, and spirit and teaches us how to listen to them, developing a true understanding of what it is we need to heal. It also builds a loving acceptance of what is so that as we take this exploratory journey we are not fighting with our reality but learning from it. It eases the tensions within us that keep us from opening our minds and hearts to listening: listening to the pain, listening to the discomfort, listening to the hope, listening to the needs, and truly hearing how we can nurture ourselves back into health. It also builds a trust of our own wisdom and knowing. We can filter out all the other stories and messages from the expectations of society, our families, our friends, our doctors, or our care takers and hear what our own being is telling us. We can take an active part in creating our own healing journey with all of the supports that fit our personal needs best.

This is not an easy task because there are many blocks within us that keep us from listening to and trusting ourselves. We have a buildup of old stories and programs that tell us to doubt ourselves and what we feel. We have developed a fear of feeling. We don't want to stay with our pain and discomfort because we might get stuck there or we don't know how to handle it. We are afraid of feeling too much happiness and joy because it feels like it doesn't actually belong and we wait for the other shoe to drop. We have old traumas and wounds that keep us from opening to certain avenues of healing. As we are building our mindful practice, we acknowledge these blocks and use our awareness to move through them all the way back to our own wisdom.

This book is meant to help you build a mindful practice that will bring you back to your own wisdom so you can discover your own healing journey. It will address some of the most common blocks that keep us from listening to ourselves and will give you practical tools on how to navigate those blocks so that you can trust the healing journey you're on. The client stories in this book are meant to help you understand the essence of the teachings. They have been altered to varying degrees to protect the individuals anonymity. Some only reflect the true story in essence but not in detail.

Reading Suggestions

This book is meant to be read slowly and intentionally. Read one chapter and then take some time to digest the material. Do the accompanying exercises several times. Journal on your responses to the questions. Implement some of the teachings into your daily life, and then move on to the next chapter. You may want to read the book once through and then return to the sections that you need more support with. You may want to record your own voice reading the exercise prompts so that you can listen to them in a relaxed meditative state. If you would like to deepen your understanding of a certain topic or get more support with the teachings, please reach out to me through my website, newleafmindfulness.com.

I

Defining Health

I

What Does Healing Mean to You?

Throughout this process of discovering your personal healing journey, you will consistently return to this question, "What does healing really mean to me?" We all have a different definition of health and what our body should be capable of doing when healthy. In our younger years this definition may be very different from the one we have as we age. We need to be aware of what our definition is in each stage of our journey and be open to it changing along the way.

We can do this by noticing what expectations we hold for our health. This can be difficult in a society that likes to tell us we have complete control over our bodies and should be fit, pain free, and beautiful all our lives. If we are struggling to do so, we are told that there is a pill we can take or a procedure we can have to get us back to that perfect body image. This can create disappointment and frustration when these things don't actually cure our physical flaws and ailments.

First, we look at the expectations we have for our body, and we notice where they came from. These expectations can be placed on us by society and the images of health portrayed to us in the media. They can be generated by our families, communities, and friends. They can be ingrained beliefs from our religion or culture. We look at how they affect the way we see ourselves and the state we are currently in. Do they make us judge ourselves? Do they make us feel guilty about what we're going through and the pain or illness we're facing? Do they tell us we're bad and wrong for being sick or injured? And we ask ourselves if these expectations are serving us in our healing.

In order to heal we must have a peaceful, accepting, and compassionate relationship with our bodies. If our definition of health is making us hate our body in the state that we're in, then we need to change our expectations. Illness and injury will happen to everyone. The longer we live, the more we will experience. This is a fact of life. No one avoids sickness, illness, and eventually death. The sooner we accept this, the sooner we will be able to start healing from these harmful expectations. We want to show ourselves grace and understanding for what we are going through and recognize that we are not alone. There is no shame in being ill or injured. We do not condemn ourselves for it.

You can use the following exercises to acknowledge the expectations you have around your health and bring more compassion and understanding to what you are going through.

1.1 HEALING OUR EXPECTATIONS AROUND HEALTH

Observing our expectations of health

Center yourself on your breath and allow it to bring your awareness back into your body.

Listen to your body as you ask the following questions.

What am I expecting my body to be able to do?

What am I expecting my body to look like?

What am I expecting my body to feel like?

How am I expecting my body to heal?

As you listen to these expectations within you, notice what relationship they are creating between you and your body. Notice what perspective they give you of your illness or injury. You can do this by asking yourself the following questions.

How do I talk to my body when I am holding it to these expectations?

How do I relate to my illness or injury when holding these expectations?

What relationship do I have with my body when holding onto these expectations?

Who does this turn me into?

How am I showing up for myself, others, and the world?

Is this helping me to heal?

Being with our illness and injury in compassion and love

Center yourself on your breath, and allow it to bring your awareness back into your body. You can place one hand over your heart and the other on the injured part of your body. Feel the loving energy of your heart center moving out into your body reaching the parts of you that are sick and unwell. Allow this flow of loving, compassionate energy to continue as you soften towards these areas.

Remind yourself that you are doing the best you know how with the information you have.

Remind yourself that your body is deserving of your love and compassion.

Put down your fight with this area of the body and offer it forgiveness and peace.

Let go of your guilt or shame around this injury.

You did not do this on purpose. You are not bad for experiencing it. You are not wrong for struggling.

You can repeat the following.

I'm sorry you are hurting. I'm sorry this is hard. My intentions are to help you heal. My intentions are to love you through this. My intentions are to listen to you and honor your needs. Help me know how to help you better. I love you, body. I love you, body.

As we let go of our harmful expectations, we come back to what is most important to us. What does healing mean to us at this phase in our lives based on our work, passions, activities, age, and needs? If, at this stage in our lives, high-intensity sports are our passion, then we may make a very different decision on a healing choice than if we are in our 80s and are all right with slowing down. If we have children to care for and raise, we may make a very different decision on our healing options. If our job requires us to travel often, we may make very different healing decisions. Again, these will be unique to each individual and will change for everyone throughout their life.

Recognizing what's most important to us will help us define health, and choose a path that will get us closest to that definition. For example, when I tore my anterior cruciate ligament (ACL) in a ski accident, I was thirty-six years old, and I loved playing in the mountains. I knew that, for me, health meant being able to hike, bike, and ski. This affected the choice I made to have reconstructive surgery rather than simply adapting to a knee without an ACL. Similarly, someone who has kids and is diagnosed with stage four cancer at age thirty may make a very different choice from someone in their 80s on the aggressiveness of care. My grandmother chose not to go through any treatment for her pancreatic cancer at age 83 because she was tired and didn't want to live her last months in ongoing medical treatment.

These choices are easier to make if we are clear on our values and what's most important to us. What is it that makes you happiest? What do you want to be capable of doing? Is it more important for you to continue doing intense activity today or protect your body for the long run? Would you rather enjoy unhealthy habits now and deal with the consequences later? How much do you care about your future health? There are no right answers. It's up to you to make the choices that fit best. This definition may change many times even in the span of reading this book. Allow it to change and adapt as you stay present and aware of what matters most to you with each new piece of information you receive and each new experience that comes into your life.

You can begin to explore your definition of health with the following exercise.

1.2 EXERCISE ON DEFINING HEALTH

Center yourself on your breath and allow it to bring your awareness back into your body. Open in non-judgmental observation as you ask yourself the following questions.

What does health mean to me?

What is most important to me at this stage of my life?

What activities and lifestyle make me happiest?

What does my profession require of me?

How do I want to show up for my family?

What does an active lifestyle mean to me?

How do I want to treat my body?

Would I rather live completely for the pleasure of today, or do I want to make choices based on my future health?

How can I feel healthy and good in my body today?

Don't make any final conclusions with these questions. Just use them to develop an understanding of what is most important to you and what might be motivating your healing choices. Again, there are no right answers.

As we come back to our own definition of health, we have to be prepared to adapt to new circumstances if we cannot attain this definition. We know that this is what we would like to work towards and we will make all of the choices necessary to get there, but sometimes it might not happen as quickly as we would like, or at all. When I was 26 years old, I ruptured a disc in my back and got nerve damage down my left leg. At that time, I was a strong athlete, always mountain biking, skiing, hiking, and climbing. After my injury, I couldn't sit in a chair without tears of pain in my eyes. My definition of health at that age was someone who could fling themselves down a mountain at high speeds without any consequences for the body, and I grieved for years the fact that I no longer could.

As time pressed on, my pain decreased, my mobility returned, and my activities increased. But after three years of healing, my definition of health had changed. I was happy just to be able to ski on intermediate runs for half a day. I was happy to take mellower bike rides and hikes that were more about the journey than the summit. I made lifestyle choices that supported this version of health for myself. I probably could have gotten a personal trainer and worked hours each day to strengthen myself to the point where I could take on the same impact as before, but I didn't feel the need. This level of activity was enough for me in my new definition of health, and I made my healing choices around that.

Ten years later, I was living in Colorado surrounded by extreme athletes who held my old definition of health. I began to want to push harder, ride farther, and ski longer. I was getting disappointed with my body because it would hurt so bad after I tried to do these things. Instead of listening, I became frustrated and unaccepting of my limitations. I pushed my body, asking it to fit this external definition of health. It couldn't maintain. My back started to flair up more often, leaving me immobile for days at a time. The pain in my back made me less stable on my skis, and I ran into a tree, tearing my ACL. My determination to heal my knee quickly, pushed me to do too much while my body was off balance, and I ruptured the same disc in my back so badly that I lost sensation and function in my right leg, resulting in the need for back surgery. Once again, my definition of health needed to adapt and modify to my new situation. What does it mean to have a capable body? Capable of what? Is being able to keep up in extreme sports really what matters most to me? Is being able to do so worth the damage it's doing to my body? We use the answers to these questions to help us make the hard choices regarding our health.

These shifts in our definition of health don't come easy. They are accompanied by a lot of denial, anger, grief, depression, and, hopefully, finally acceptance. But, as I have experienced, acceptance sometimes reverts back to denial and we relapse into old definitions of health that don't actually serve us. Then we start all over again. This is an ongoing process that we experience with grace, forgiveness, and understanding. We know that our body will constantly be changing and adapting to our new experiences and situations and that we will have to adapt with it.

Striving for our definition of health is a positive thing, because it motivates us to take care of ourselves and make choices that serve us best. However, we have to be realistic with these definitions and allow them to change when need be so that we can bring love and acceptance to where our body is in this moment. We learn to listen to our illness and understand the lifestyle changes it is asking us to make. In honoring the needs of the body, we may discover new sides of ourselves that we were too distracted by activity to acknowledge before. We may find that our new lifestyle fits us even better and allows us to express new passions and interests and that these allow us to show up as the best version of ourselves out in the world.

We will explore more of this process as the book continues, but for now we will open ourselves to accepting that our body may not meet our old definitions of health. This allows us to move forward in our healing journey in a way that best serves our overall well-being.

1.3 EXERCISE ON ACCEPTING THE CHANGES IN OUR BODY

Center yourself on your breath and allow it to bring your awareness back into your body. Open in nonjudgmental observation as you observe your current relationship with your body.

Notice what definition of health you are holding your body to right now. Notice your expectations around your healing: the timing, the process, and the outcome. Look at where you are trying to arrive in your healing journey. What are you hoping to feel like, look like, or perform like after you heal?

Now release these expectations and come back to your experience right here and right now. What are you experiencing in your body in this moment? What is your body capable of in this moment? What does your body need in this moment? Can you be at peace with where your body is right here and right now?

Can you carry the peace and acceptance you feel with your body in this moment into the next one, and the next, and into the future? Can you give your body permission to live this experience at its own pace? Can you be open to shifting your definition of health if it turns out that your old expectations can't be met? Can you still love your body even if you don't achieve the healing results you were hoping for?

Repeat the following: I love my body in every state that it's in. I know my body is doing the best that it can in this moment, in this situation, with the information I have and the tools I've been given. My intentions are to do my best to listen to and honor the needs of my body even if they don't match my previous expectations.

Most definitions of health now include our whole being: mind, body, and spirit. But what does this really mean? So many opinions exist on how this connection works and how to get all these parts functioning well together. There are many beliefs on the varying ranges of influence each of these pieces has and which one to focus on to heal them all. I have heard and seen success stories for varying approaches and can't say there is a right answer. I have used methods that focus more on one or the other and have had success and failure. I am part of a healing collective with practitioners who focus on different components of the whole being, and each one has a different perspective and view on which one will actually heal us. This comes back to the importance of self-awareness and developing the ability to listen to ourselves. What does this mind-body-spirit connection mean to you?

We know that our mental and emotional world influences our physical one by affecting our nervous system and, in turn, what bodily functions get turned on or off. We also know that our spiritual world influences our perception of reality, which alters our emotions and mental states, and, in turn, our physical body. We know that our beliefs around our healing change the way we heal. Yet there is still no one-size fits-all program that will bring everyone back into a healthy balanced state. It's up to each individual to create the healing journey that will work best for them.

In my own healing journey, I have been told that my physical state was simply a mental and emotional issue. My lethargy, migraine headaches, decreased lung capacity, and anal bleeding was labeled a result of depression. This was the medical world's explanation for something they did not know the answer to. Yet, after months of testing because I refused to accept this, a biopsy finally showed that I had Schistosomiasis, a parasite that I had contracted from Ghana that lived in my lungs and created egg sacks that traveled through the circulatory system attaching to the capillaries and cutting off oxygen exchange in my organs. After taking horse de-wormer and detoxing for months, I started to return to my healthy self.

I have also experienced migraine headaches that begin when I am putting too much pressure on myself and feel like I have to defend myself by going into fight mode. This creates vascular tension within my body because my sympathetic nervous system has taken over and creates narrow vision and headaches. In these moments, self-awareness, deep breathing, and meditation are what help me most. This physical ailment really is caused by imbalances in my emotional world.

There are also mind-body connections that are deeply ingrained and alter the way we function in the world. Our physical ailments could be very real, like my torn ACL, yet they still have an emotional, mental, and spiritual component. My beliefs around my self-worth and what I should be capable of push me to act in ways that compromise my health. I make the choice to ski harder instead of calling it a day because I don't want to appear weak or unfun. This is based on my definition of self-worth and what I believe I have to do in order to be accepted.

My back pain was a complicated, unclear mix of all the physical, mental, and emotional realms. When the pain first began, it was caused by my method of releasing emotional trauma. The pain from emotional abuse in my past was held in my body and the only way that I could find reprieve from it was to push myself to the limits in my sports. Physical exertion that inflicted pain on my body was my way of expressing the stuck emotional pain within me. This led to the choices that ended up rupturing my disc.

My fear of not having the support that I needed and a skepticism of the western medical system led me to alternative methods of healing. After three years of energy work, meditation, emotional work, and alternative body work, my back pain began to ease. I did address the emotional traumas held in those muscles, and I could feel them tightening or loosening depending on how much I was trusting myself and feeling safe in the world. I saw that when my emotional world was more peaceful, my body became peaceful. My body thanked me for not taking out my mental and emotional distress on it. This gave me great confidence that I could remedy my back pain with mental and emotional work.

The practitioners that I frequented reflected this mentality to me. They gave me literature and lectures on how back pain is linked to our emotions, that it is only there to distract us from the emotional traumas we don't want to deal with. They encouraged me to stop altering my behavior based on the pain and stop limiting myself out of fear. These are easier arguments to make with back pain because it still remains an unsolved mystery with no great scientific remedy. Surgery has only a 50% success rate and many people who have surgery return for more in the future. Some people have the same amount of pain, if not more, after surgery and lose even more nerve function. When there is no clear answer, the uncertainty pushes us to come to our own conclusions so that we have a semblance of control.

I wanted to believe that I could manage my pain injury by nurturing my emotional world. As my desire to do all of my usual extreme sports returned, I wanted to believe that I could because there was no actual physical problem with my back. If I believed it and stopped putting energy towards the injury, maybe it would go away. I so badly wanted to free myself of the limitations of my back. This mentality was fed by the practitioners I frequented. But this in itself is a form of mental abuse that will lead to injury. It convinces us not to listen to and honor the needs of our body. It convinces us that we can will ourselves back into being capable if we just stop believing in our injury. When I listened to my back and believed it, I adapted my lifestyle to support it. Once I stopped wanting to believe it, my old habits of wanting to push myself in all areas of my life returned, and the injury had to manifest even larger until I was forced to take more drastic medical means to resolve it.

Yes, my emotional and mental world had a huge impact on my back health, but the physical manifestation of the injury was just as real and needed just as much nurturing. There is no doubt that there is an inseparable connection between our physical, mental, emotional, and spiritual worlds, but we cannot solve all of them by only addressing one. We have to acknowledge and nurture the needs of each part of us.

This is the same for people who have stress-related illnesses. Yes, their cancer or autoimmune disease is an actual physical manifestation within the body that needs to be addressed, but there are also emotional, mental, and spiritual states that took part in their formation. If we feel insecure about our value in the world and need to prove our worth by doing more and achieving more, we will put ourselves into lifestyle and work situations that are highly demanding and strenuous. This will then increase our stress and decrease our immune system. If we feel like we are responsible for taking care of everyone else and that making them happy is the only way to keep ourselves safe, then we will overcommit ourselves and deplete our own system.

Being aware of these connections helps us to learn more from our ailments and use them to teach us how to live in ways that serve us better. We can listen to the ailment and what lifestyle changes it is asking us to make, and honor those so that we can live as our healthiest selves. **In order to make these lifestyle changes, we will need to shift in our mental and spiritual world because we will probably need to redefine where our worth comes from, what success means, or what it looks like to show up well for others.**

I had a client who had a job coordinating linguistic projects in Africa. Her self-worth was linked to this job in so many ways. It confirmed her spiritual worth because her work was religiously motivated. It confirmed her personal worth because she was important and valued in her position. It confirmed her strength because she was able to put herself into very taxing situations and survive. But it was taking a toll on her health. She had horrible varicose veins and hemorrhoids that would flair up every time she had to take those long flights. She was constantly on de-worming medications for the worms she would get in her digestive tract. Her blood pressure was extremely high, and she had respiratory issues. These were all real physical problems within her body, but her mental and spiritual state were preventing her from addressing them. She wanted to be able to continue her work even though it was deteriorating her body.

We began to shift her perspective on where her worth came from and what her purpose was. We began to shift what it meant to be spiritual, letting go of the idea that her religion had to be her work. We came back to what was really important to her, being able to show up as a loving, peaceful, and compassionate presence for others which her illnesses were not allowing her to do. This allowed her to shift her view of self, and, in turn, her priorities. She quit her job and began her healing journey. She spent a lot of time getting the medical attention she needed for her ailments, but what allowed these procedures to work this time, when they hadn't before, was the fact that her lifestyle now supported the self-care necessary to maintain her health. If she had simply returned to her old lifestyle and her old beliefs, all of her ailments would have returned.

Our balance between mind, body, and spirit is always changing relative to our circumstances and experiences. Each time we face a new illness or injury the parts of us that need more nurturing and attention may be different. This is why mindful awareness of our own internal state is so important. It helps us to observe what is going on in our whole system and listen to what we need in order to come back to center. We then reach out for the support we need to do so.

We can begin by simply acknowledging the mind-body-spirit connection and getting used to listening to all three. We can create our own interpretation of what this connection means to us and how we can support ourselves as whole beings.

1.4 EXERCISES ON RECOGNIZING YOUR MIND-BODY-SPIRIT CONNECTION

Center yourself on your breath and allow it to bring your awareness back into your body. Feel your body in this moment. What is your body experiencing right now? What does it feel like to be present in your body? Ask the body what it's struggling with right now. You may get back in touch with your pain or illness. Hold a hand here and then ask the following questions.

How is this affecting my mental well-being?

How does my mental state affect this physical experience?

Are the struggles in my mental world manifesting in my physical body?

Do I treat my body differently because of my mental state?

How is this affecting my emotional well-being?

How does my emotional state affect this physical experience?

Are my unaddressed emotional needs manifesting in my physical body?

Do I treat my body differently because of my emotional state?

How is this affecting my spiritual well-being?

How does my spiritual state affect this physical experience?

Is my spiritual unrest or disconnect manifesting in my physical body?

Do I treat my body differently because of my spiritual state?

There is nothing to solve or fix here. Simply observe and start feeling the connection between your whole being. You are mental, emotional, spiritual, and physical, and all of these parts of you work together to generate your experience in this world.

2

Settling

2

Settling the body

When our bodies are unwell we experience turmoil in our physical, mental, and spiritual world. Our anxiety and worry rise, maybe we experience anger and frustration; maybe we feel grief and depression. This creates an unsettling in our spiritual world as we stop trusting ourselves, and sometimes we stop trusting whatever greater force we believed in. This puts us into a stress state which takes its own toll on our physical well-being. We are now spending more time in our sympathetic nervous system, which decreases our ability to metabolize food and absorb nutrients, slows our cell regeneration, decreases our oxygen intake, depletes our immune system, and stresses our heart. None of these things are beneficial to our healing. This is why our first step to healing is settling. Bringing ourselves back into a state of peace so that we can rest and recuperate.

The easiest way to settle our internal state is to breathe. The breath is directly tied to our autonomic nervous system which is in charge of switching us between the sympathetic and parasympathetic modes. The vagus nerve runs through the diaphragm and sends signals through our system indicating our state based on how we're breathing. If we are breathing shallow and fast, then the vagus nerve is telling us that we are stressed. If our breathing is slow, deep, and steady, then the vagus nerve sends a signal back saying that we are calm and restful. This signal is most often enough to switch us back into our parasympathetic nervous system, allowing us to rest, replenish, and rebuild.

The breath also reminds us that we are not alone in this world. We remember that all other living beings participate in the same process of oxygen exchange either in the same direction of oxygen in and CO_2 out, or CO_2 in and oxygen out. We also see that all of the elements present in the world around us are also present within us. This decreases the separation between us and the world around us, reminding us that by taking care of our external world, we are taking care of our internal one. This can also remind us of how much bigger than us this whole story is and how we are just one of the many working parts in this beautiful complex system. We start to perceive this system with gratitude, recognizing what a miracle it is to be alive experiencing this gift. If we are breathing, we are still alive, and what a gift that is.

The following breathing exercises will help you begin settling your nervous system returning to a state of rest. They were taken from my book *Living From the Heart*.

2.1 BREATHING EXERCISES

Feeling the breath

Place all of your attention on the breath and follow the sensations from where the air enters your nose to how it fills the diaphragm. You may feel that the air is cooler when it enters and warmer when it exits. You may feel the slight movement of the hairs on your upper lip or the slight flare of the nostrils as air passes. You may feel the slight opening of the throat as it allows air to pass or the rise and fall of the chest.

As you pull the air deeper into the body, you may feel the expansion of the stomach and the side ribs and out into the back. You may feel the slight contraction as the belly button pulls back towards the spine and you gently squeeze out any remaining air in the lungs.

Find the place within the process of breathing that holds your attention best and continually bring you focus back to it anytime the mind wanders.

5-5-7 breathing

Breathe in for five seconds, hold the breath for five seconds, and breathe out for seven seconds. Pause at the bottom of the exhale and breathe out a little bit more before breathing back in.

Count your breaths

Count each in-breath and out-breath. Each time your mind wanders, bring your attention back to the breath and start at one. This is done in non-judgment. We do not judge when the mind wanders; we gently guide it back to the breath.

When our body is in pain or ill, we may feel anger and frustration towards the body. We may be resisting our experience and fighting with our illness. This anger and fight only leads to more tension in the body, which increases our stress and decreases our ability to heal. In order to settle the body and bring it back to peace, we need to make peace with our experience. It may not be a pleasant experience. No one enjoys being sick or injured. Yet it will happen to all of us at one point in our lives. No one avoids these experiences, and fighting them only harms us more. **Acknowledging the discomfort of our situation and bringing acceptance to it is the first step to finding peace in the body.**

In order to acknowledge what we are experiencing in the body we have to be present for it. We form many techniques to avoid our discomfort. We consume mind-altering substances. We consume media. We distract ourselves with work and tasks. We put ourselves constantly in the presence of others so that we don't have to be alone in our own experience. But the experience is still in the background, nagging at us and irritating our internal state. It doesn't disappear because we don't look at it. So, our first step is to learn how to look and listen.

Us humans have become very cerebral creatures, and we

spend most of our time in our heads. Even if we are experiencing something in our physical form, we spend more time trying to explain why we are feeling it and how we could fix it than simply feeling what we are feeling. At any point, the body is receiving over 11 billion sensory inputs. Yet our mind only processes about nine of those at once. Most of the time, we are completely unaware of what the body is feeling. This is not all bad; if we had to consciously process 11 billion pieces of information at once, we would never get anything else done. But when our body is experiencing an imbalance, manifesting as pain and illness, it becomes more crucial to pay attention to and learn from these feelings in the body.

Learning to listen means bringing our attention away from our mind's reaction to sensation and back into the sensations themselves, perceiving them without judgment or the desire to change. We even try not to label them at all—just feel. Many of us go through our day without once feeling our ankle, toe, or elbow. Unless a body part hurts, we don't remember that we have it and that it is serving us in each moment. Feeling the body means remembering every body part and the crucial role they play in our health and ability to participate in this life. It means acknowledging that they are all feeling many sensations all the time and that this is how they know what to do for us at each moment.

As we tune into these sensations, we feel grateful for all the body does to keep us alive, healthy, and balanced. We recognize that being aware of what the body is going through helps us to know how to take better care of it. If our back hurts, we may need to change our posture or stand up and walk around. If our head hurts, we may need to take a break from our screen. If we are breathing shallow we may need to take three deep breaths. If we weren't paying attention, we wouldn't know that the body needed these things and we would continue on with the activities or habits that were harming it, leading to more serious illness or injury.

These exercises will help you to tune into your body and feel what it's experiencing. They were taken from my book, *Living from the Heart.*

2.2 EXERCISES ON PAYING ATTENTION TO THE BODY

Tuning into our senses

Sit in a quiet peaceful place and allow your mind to settle. Once you are focused inward, clap your hands. Use some force and stiff hands so that you create a strong sensation. Hold the hands about four inches apart and tune all of your awareness to the sensations in them.

Observe with curiosity as though you were experiencing touch for the first time. Try not to label, judge, or tell a story; just feel. Notice if the sensation is different in different spots on the hand.

Then change your focus to just one small spot on one hand. It may be one fingertip or one place in the center of the palm. Place all of your attention here. Notice if the sensation in this one spot is different from the overall sensation in the hand.

Does focusing on this one spot change your experience of the sensations elsewhere in the hand?

Now bring your focus back wide and see if you can find the sensation that you felt in that one spot elsewhere in the hands. Begin to observe as the sensation fades away. How is it evolving over time? What sensation is left when the one we created is gone?

Then widen your focus even further. Can you feel the same baseline sensation of aliveness that you found in the hands elsewhere in the body? Maybe this tingling or this vibration of life. This is the feeling of being awake and aware.

Now you can bring your hands together to touch. Really be with the feeling of them touching one another. Does it feel different now than it normally does because you are so aware of it? Play with moving the hand and fingers and feeling every sensation of movement.

Now allow your hands to rest on your lap as they settle back into a normal state, but keep your awareness alive to all the sensations in your body. This is what it feels like to be connected with sensation.

Body Scan

This is a body scan meditation to get you in touch with what is going on in your physical form. You will approach the sensations in your body with open and accepting awareness. You may want to lie down on your back with your knees and head supported by a cushion.

Allow your whole body to relax, giving every muscle permission to stop supporting you as you give your weight over to the earth. You can feel the earth softening beneath you, molding to the weight of your body. You can begin the scan by becoming aware of your internal organs and systems that keep you alive and functioning every day: your lungs, digestive system, detoxing organs, and heart. Send recognition and gratitude to each one.

Then your sense organs, eyes, tongue, ears, nose, and skin. What a miracle to be able to sense the world around us.

Now you can start your scan of the body, beginning at the feet. Acknowledge each part of the body, identifying with any sensation you find there. Observe without judgment, without telling a story, and without trying to fix. Right now we just notice and realize that every experience, good or bad, is a part of this great gift of being alive.

If your mind gets stuck in areas of tension or pain, use the breath to move it forward onto another part of the body. Travel through the whole body, part by part, before bringing the whole body into your awareness, recognizing that each part is one piece of the integral whole. Reunite the body all together, leaving no part out, and send gratitude all through it.

When we are in the middle of an illness or injury, tuning into the sensations of the body may be really difficult because what we find is unpleasant. When this is the case, we start with all the body parts that don't hurt, with everything that is going well in our body. We try to remember that we are more than our illness. We remember that if we are still breathing, we are still alive and that is the greatest gift we could ever receive.

We continue to do the body scan in this way until we feel a more peaceful connection with the body and are able to focus on more than just our pain or illness. This is very important so that, when we start paying attention to the illness, we do not get overwhelmed and stuck in depression because of what isn't working. Any time we are acknowledging the pain within us, we can easily turn back to the remembrance of the body as a miracle and all the good things it does for us in each moment. We remember that even if the body is not perfect, it is still here connecting us to the world around us, giving us this experience of life.

In order to prepare for acknowledging our bodily suffering, it helps to redevelop our trust of the body. **We remember that, although the body is ailing, it wants to be whole, healthy, and balanced and it knows how to get itself back there. We remember that it carries its own wisdom into what it needs to be well and, if we just listen, it will do its best to get us there.** By making a peaceful and stable environment for the body in which we are able to listen to it and honor its needs, we can help it to do its healing work.

You can use the following exercises to remember what a miracle the body is. These exercises were taken from my book *Living from the Heart.*

2.3 EXERCISES ON TRUSTING THE BODY

Seeing the body as a miracle

You can do this exercise following a Body Scan (explained above). Once you are in contact with each part of the body and the body is reunited within your consciousness, begin to give gratitude towards it.

Recognize all the things your body does for you. Recognize how it keeps you alive and how it allows you to connect with the world and act within it. Acknowledge all of the miraculous activities you are able to do.

Understand that in loving the body, you are loving all of creation. In loving the body, you are giving gratitude to life. Know that your body was created for a specific purpose and that you are made in the divine nature. You are divine. In accepting the body, we accept the divine and step into our purpose. Love your body.

Trusting the body's ability to heal

This exercise can follow the previous one or can be done on its own after a body scan. Find the areas of the body that trouble you. If you do not have any physical pain or illness, then identify the areas of the body that you are unhappy with or want to change.

Place a hand over this area of the body.

What is the body asking for?

How does it need to be nurtured?

Working from your heart space, offer the body what it needs. Allow the difficult area back into the whole body so that it is connected into the whole. Identify with the body's ability to heal.

Listen to the body's deepest desire to be whole and healthy. Trust that the body can heal. Encourage the body to heal.

Tell the body that you are here to help it heal itself. Visualize the body healing itself, reconstructing, rewiring, clearing, cleansing, and detoxing.

Believe that the body can heal. Visualize the body healing for as long as you can, as many times a day as you can. Offer healing energies throughout the entire body.

Stay with the belief that the body can heal. Offer love to the body. Repeat the follow, "Thank you body for all that you do to keep me alive, balanced, and well. I believe that you are capable of healing. I trust that you know how to heal. I trust that you will heal."

Now that we remember that the body is a miracle and is

doing its best to heal, we can acknowledge the suffering of the body. In this acknowledgment, we are not looking for a solution or trying to fix it. We are not trying to find the reason that it's here and judging it. We are simply observing what it feels like in the body and admitting that it hurts, that it is hard, that it is causing suffering in our physical form. As long as we are denying our pain and our illness, it cannot receive the energy it needs to heal.

There are many reasons that we may be denying our physical experience, and we will touch on some of those later, but essentially it is because we don't want it to be here for one reason or another. We perceive it to be a nuisance here to sabotage our lives and stop us in our tracks. We see all the things it will take away from us, the relationships it will strain, the job it will threaten, the money it will suck up, and the negative image it will create of us. This perspective does not include the whole truth. Yes, these things may happen in our lives, but they do not need to create a negative reality for us. There is much more to this story.

Maybe this will move us in a new direction that is healthier for us. Maybe we will start prioritizing things that actually bring us happiness. Maybe we will develop a lifestyle that serves us and our loved ones better. Maybe we will learn new skills and passions while we are moving slower. Maybe we will deepen our spiritual self. There are many other possibilities for this experience that don't have to be negative. **Even though we have been trained to believe that pain and illness are nothing but bad, we don't have to believe it. This experience too belongs in our lives and will serve its own purpose on our larger growth journey.**

This is the wonderful Buddhist teaching of no mud, no lotus. The beautiful lotus flower grows only in mud. Without the mud, it would not exist. This is true of all things in life. The good would not exist without the bad. Rebirth would not happen without death. Light cannot shine without darkness. We know that this is true, and yet every time something difficult happens in our lives, we forget the flower that it will produce. If we keep our perspective on the bigger picture, on the growth, on the learning, then the flower will start to grow in our mud. It might not grow right away and it does not take away all of the suffering, but it does help us to maintain our intentions through the difficult moments. It reminds us who we want to be in the world and how we want to use every experience to develop more peace, more compassion, and more love.

These deeper intentions are held within our heart space. This is the core of our being, where our deeper wisdom lies. Where we hold a connection with all of life and recognize our part in the greater system. It is this heart space that helps us to develop an understanding of our situation that is larger than just the temporary loss or pain. It sees the growth that can manifest and how we can use that growth to better serve the world around us. Holding onto these intentions, we can look at our suffering without falling down a dark hole of despair. We can admit this is hard without wallowing in the negative. Yes, this is difficult. Yes, it is hard when our body is not functioning as we would like. And, yes, we will grow a lotus from this mud.

You can use the following exercises to help you come back to your intentions for every experience and acknowledge what you are struggling with now.

2.4 EXERCISES ON KNOWING YOUR INTENTIONS AND ACKNOWLEDGING YOUR PAIN

Remembering your intentions

You can start with a breathing and settling exercise. Bring your awareness back into the body and center on your heart space. This core of your being is nothing but love, peace, compassion, acceptance and gratitude.

Remember what it is that this heart space values most. What is most important to it? What do you truly want to prioritize? Who do you want to be out in the world and how do you want to show up for yourself, others, and the world?

How does this heart space see this experience of pain or illness?

What does this heart space know about the bigger truth?

How does this heart space want you to use this experience for your growth?

What does this heart space want you to focus on while you are going through this?

What does this heart space want you to be cultivating within yourself through this struggle?

Does your heart space and the greater wisdom see this experience as all bad?

Where does it see your lotus growing?

Visualize your lotus flower beginning to bloom through the mud of this experience. Set your intentions to use this experience to grow and transform and continue living as your true self.

Acknowledging what hurts

You can start with a breathing and settling exercise. Bring your awareness back into the body and center on your heart space. This core of your being that's nothing but love, peace, compassion, acceptance, and gratitude.

Remember that this heart space can hold every experience in our lives with love, compassion, and understanding. It is the heart that can heal all things.

In trust of the heart, know that you can admit what you are struggling with without fear or overwhelm. You can acknowledge your pain and be with it in peace.

With the love of the heart, you can begin to acknowledge what hurts or is ailing in the body.

What is your body feeling that hurts?

What feels out of balance in your body?

Where is the illness in your body?

What effects is this having on your physical form and the activities you are capable of?

Is it limiting you?

What is hard about this for you?

What does it bring up for you?

You can continue to move through these questions over and over until you get the whole truth of what your body is going through right now. It might go deeper than the surface ailment and go into how the body is compensating and the effects of that. It might go into the effects of the treatments you are using. It might go into the effects of the limitations it has put on you. Allow yourself to truly admit all sides of this experience and how they affect the body.

Now that we have acknowledged what we are experiencing in our body, we can make peace with it. We cannot heal if we are at war with our body, trying to fight what is. The fight creates the stress state that sucks our energy from healing. Peace comes with acceptance.

Acceptance is not the same thing as complacency. It does not mean that we turn over and give up on trying to make change. Acceptance allows us to be with what is happening in our lives with an open mind and heart. It says, "This too belongs and has a purpose on my journey and I am excited to find out what that is." It turns us into a curious observer of our situation and this state is what allows us to see clearly. If we are fogged by anger and judgment and fighting, we are looking at things through a tainted lens and we cannot see any of the open pathways out. Acceptance opens our space so that we can see all of the doors still available to us and all the different ways we can choose to walk through them towards healing.

We recognize that no one is doing this to us. The body is not out to get us or sabotaging our lives on purpose. We are not the only ones who have to experience pain and illness and who suffer from it. This is a natural occurrence in life and, if we live long enough and full enough, it will definitely happen to all of us in many different forms and in many different ways. Acceptance says, "I accept that this is a part of my journey and I am open to being present for it so that I can grow into a truer version of myself." It helps us to not spend all our time feeling sorry for ourselves and moves us toward positive action.

One of my clients spent years denying the pain in her stomach and the increased bleeding around her period. She denied it because she held herself responsible for holding everyone else's life together. She thought the world could not continue to function without her, so she could not take a break to deal with this health issue; therefore, it couldn't be there. It took her years to start to acknowledge that it was actually there, causing much pain and anguish in her daily life. It took her even longer to let go of the need to solve everyone else's problems long enough to take care of herself. As she stepped out of the role of fixer and solver, she gave herself the freedom to look into her own pain and acknowledge that it needed some attention. Her acceptance of the situation allowed her to stop fighting the fact that she was in pain and find a path out. She ended up having surgery and taking four weeks off of her busy life and found herself pain-free and guilt-free for the first time in decades. The experience helped her to take one more step towards honoring her own needs instead of only focusing on fixing others. She is still on a healing journey, but this illness was a catalyst to one important change on her path.

You can use the following exercises to make peace with the pain and illness within you. This is a modification from an exercise in my book Living from the Heart.

2.5 EXERCISES ON MAKING PEACE WITH PAIN AND ILLNESSES

Accepting our illness and pain

This exercise should also be done after a Body Scan so that you are in contact with each part of the body in non-judgmental awareness. You can then place your attention on the areas of your body where you feel tension, sickness, or pain. If you do not have any physical pain or illness, then identify the areas of the body that you are unhappy with or want to change.

Place a hand over this area of the body. Listen to how you communicate with this area.

What are you saying to it?

How do your words feel?

How does the body react to them?

What are you asking it to do?

How do you see it?

Are you fighting with it?

Are you pushing it away and denying it?

Do you feel any guilt or shame because it is there?

Is this really how you want to interact with the body?

What would the body rather hear from you?

Can you see this ailment as an equal part of you?

Now be with the pain, illness, or imperfection in love. See if you can take down the boundaries around the difficult area. Soften around it so that you give it room to breathe and move. See if you can soften its edges so that it is no longer a solid defined object. Allow it to dissipate outwards as you widen your awareness further and further.

As your attention widens, the difficult area seems less dominant. It melts into the rest of the body, no longer a separate self but included within the whole. The fighting subsides as it is held by the body.

The body can now share its healing energies with itself. Allow the flow of energy to enter into it, washing the pain away and reintegrating it into the harmonious system.

Notice how this opens your perspective from what is wrong with our body and life and onto all of the possibilities for growth and healing. You can begin to see all of your paths towards healing instead of all of your limitations. You can choose to move towards these new paths, no longer stuck in the fight with what is.

3

Settling the mind

When we have a part of the body that is painful or ill it occupies a lot of our mind space. It is the constant background noise for everything else we are doing. We are speaking to someone, and half of our mind is focused on what they are saying while the other half is dealing with the nagging pain in us or the fear of our illness. We are trying to accomplish a task, and half of our mind is focused on the actions while the other half is worried about how it will affect that body part or how the illness is making it more difficult. I myself experience this with my back pain. When it gets really bad, I recognize that as my partner is speaking, I'm irritated that he keeps talking when what I really need to do is go lie down. While I'm driving I am literally a danger because the pain keeps me from focusing on the road, and all I want is to get where I'm going so I don't have to sit anymore. Essentially our pain and illness keeps us from being present with where we are.

Mindfulness means that we are present here and now. When we are ill, this may simply mean that we notice our mind in this moment is partially on our pain or illness and partially on what is right in front of us. We notice how this will affect our presence in the world. We recognize how tiring it is to have this in our mind playing on repeat. Mindfulness gives us the awareness of where the mind goes throughout the day, and it also gives us a reprieve from that busy cluttered mind.

We will start by giving ourselves a break from the busy cluttered mind. In order to heal our perception of our illness and our mind's relationship to it, we must first create space from it. If we are stuck in our negative thought patterns telling us how bad this is and how it will never get better, then we can't bring in healing. Some of us may not even be aware of how often we think of our illness. The thoughts taint our everyday perspective and then we don't know why we are acting cruel to the people we love or why we are unable to focus at work. In order to understand what thoughts we are having and how they are affecting us, we first have to slow them down enough so we can listen.

You can begin with these exercises that help you create a distance from your thoughts, giving you the opportunity to observe them rather than engage with them and follow their story line. You can also accomplish this by doing the breathing exercises in chapter one. The first exercise simply invites you to observe your immediate surroundings. When we place our attention on the sensory input around us, it gives us something to focus on other than our thoughts. The second exercise helps you to begin to observe your thoughts without judgment. We approach our thoughts with curiosity. We simply want to know where the mind goes right now, not change it. These exercises are from my book, *Living from the Heart.*

3.1 EXERCISES ON OBSERVING THE MIND

Watching thoughts

You should begin with a simple breathing exercise, coming back to the breath and allowing it to settle your mind and relax your body.

Once you are centered and calm, take your awareness up into your mind. Create a wide open space in the mind. You may imagine it as an open field with soft grasses and a clear blue sky overhead.

Recognize this as the natural state of the mind: open, non-judgmental, and observing. From this place of peace, begin to watch your thoughts as though they were clouds drifting through the sky.

Know that your thoughts, just like the clouds, are all made of the same elements that come together in a certain way for a specific moment and then shift, transform, and disappear as the elements change form.

Your thoughts, like the clouds, are never permanent. They come and go, shift and change. The only thing that remains constant is the natural state of the clear blue sky behind them, open and observing everything that manifests in non-judgmental awareness.

Notice how the clouds manifest into different shapes and sizes. Some are light and wispy, barely holding a shape. Others are bright and attractive like the clouds of a sunset. Some are fluffy and friendly, fun to look at, and creative. Some are dark and scary, enveloping the whole sky and seemingly all-encompassing. But no matter what their shape, they all have one thing in common: they will change, transform, move on, and eventually disappear.

Your thoughts are the same. They are different in content but the same in nature. Even the darkest of thoughts will eventually soften and dissipate into rain or into clear sky. No mental state lasts forever.

We find comfort in their impermanence and ever-changing nature. We can allow them to manifest and exist without grasping at them or pushing them away. They will come and go naturally as we rest back in peace.

Be in your surroundings

Sit in a pleasant place and tune into your senses one at a time. Give them your full attention.

Be with the sense of sound. Listen as though you were hearing things for the first time. Don't judge. Don't tell a story. Just listen.

Then tune into your sense of smell. Smell with curiosity.

Then tune into your sense of touch. Don't create new sensations, just pay attention to the ones you already have. Feel the breeze, the hair on your neck, and the fabric on your skin.

Then open your eyes and look as though you were seeing for the first time. Don't judge. Don't name. Just enjoy the shapes, colors, and contrasts.

Be fully present for your surroundings.

Now we want to start noticing where the mind goes when it's wandering away from the present moment. These thoughts usually repeat themselves and don't really tell us anything of value. The negative ones remind us what we're afraid of, what we're worrying about, what we have to fix, what we regret. We may be judging our surroundings, labeling everything and everyone as good or bad, right or wrong. We may be judging our experiences as fair or unfair. We may also be thinking about what we enjoyed yesterday or what we hope will happen tomorrow and everything we have to do to guarantee that it will happen. All of these thoughts occupy our mind space and keep us from really hearing the wisdom of our mind, body, and spirit. They are the busy-ness of the mind that distracts us from the deeper feelings and intuitions. These are the thoughts that we want to notice and help settle.

We notice each of our thoughts and recognize which ones repeat themselves most often. Some of our most troublesome thoughts will play on repeat over and over, convincing us of their truth. They may determine how we see ourselves, others, and the world, influencing our perception of reality. If we have a belief that everyone is out to get us, then we will constantly be on the lookout for examples of that truth. If we believe that we never have enough, then we will never engage with abundance.

This then influences who we are being and how we treat ourselves, others, and the planet. The belief of never having enough may make us envious of those who have more and lead to us taking advantage of others or being selfish, which in turn will make others want to help us less and will increase our perception of lack. The belief that everyone is out to get us may lead to us being defensive and guarded always quick to fight, which in turn will make others less agreeable towards us, confirming our perception of the negative other.

As we observe, we do so in non-judgment. We are not here to condemn ourselves for what goes on in our mind, we are simply here to understand. Understanding our thoughts helps us to discover why we experience life the way we do. We recognize that our thoughts are not the whole truth and that we can choose to let them go. Every time we see one of our thoughts, we recognize it, acknowledge its presence, and then let it go. No need to carry on with the story. No need to believe it and follow it down the rabbit hole. Just see it and let go. This is such a freeing experience to realize that we are not your thoughts and that our thoughts can shift and change.

We don't have to fight with our mind and the thoughts that it has. Our minds are a miraculous gift that we were given to process life, plan for the future, learn from the past, dream, and create. They are not our enemy. They have given us the gift of progress, growth, connection, and invention. We just have to learn how to use them to lift us up instead of sink us into depression, regret, and judgment.

Our goal is not to have an empty mind, but to train our attention to be mindful of what will be most helpful to us instead of cluttering itself with thoughts that simply distract us. We do this not by trying to push these thoughts away and judge them, but by becoming the curious observer, developing an understanding of what these thoughts are and what they do to our internal state. This understanding will make it easier for us to let go of the thoughts that don't serve us and redirect our attention to what serves us better.

It is in a quiet mind that we are able to hear what our pain and illness are really saying and needing. Without the quiet, all we can hear are our own fears and stories about our experience—spending our time resenting what is happening to us instead of listening to what is needed to emerge from it a fuller, happier person.

We can begin this process by simply watching our thoughts and observing the effect they have on our internal state. We can then focus on the thoughts we are having about our pain or illness, noticing what type of reaction these thoughts are creating within us. Are they motivating us to nurture and love ourselves in ways that help us heal or are they filling us with fear and anger around our experience? If they don't serve us, can we let them go? Recognize that we are so much more than our thoughts and we don't have to believe everything they are saying, especially if they are creating negativity within us. You can do this with the following exercises.

3.2 EXERCISES ON OBSERVING OUR THOUGHTS

Noticing where the mind goes

You can begin with a breathing exercise and then step into that clear open space behind thought.

From this space of non-judgmental awareness, begin to watch your thoughts and where they go. Watch as they manifest and then watch your urge to give them importance and follow them away.

Instead of following the thought, just notice if it was in the past, the present, or the future and label it accordingly. Continue this way for a minute.

Once you feel that you are able to watch the thoughts without following them, you can begin to notice what reaction the thought produces. Watch the thought, know if it is in the past, present, or future, and then name what it brings up in you: anxiety, the need to do, urgency, peace, love, sadness, or blaming.

Don't judge these reactions, just notice that the thought is generating them within you. Instead of following the thought and the reaction it produces, come back to your breath and that open space.

Your thought was of that nature, but you are of the nature of open space and peace. See the difference between your state and the state of your thoughts. They are not the same. Allow your thoughts to continue coming and going as you rest in that peaceful space.

Recognizing our story around illness or pain

Please begin this exercise with a body scan connecting with the whole body. Find the areas of the body that trouble you.

Place a hand over this area of the body. Listen to the story you tell yourself about this ailment, injury or imperfection.

Are you feeding the fear story?

Are you generating more limitations for yourself by telling limiting stories? Do you hold negative energy in this area by labeling it as bad or unfixable?

Are you fearful of making certain movements? Do you tell yourself not to do certain things because they may make things worse?

Are you focused on all of your limitations and everything you have lost?

Is there stress stored here? Is there anger or resentment stored here?

Are these stories helping you heal?

Can you let go of these negative stories?

Can you replace them with an attitude of peace and acceptance?

Can you place your thoughts on your healing and growth?

Notice what this does for your relationship to this part of the body. You may tell it something like, "I know that you are hurting. I'm here for you. I know that there are many things you are still capable of and I am grateful to you. I am here to support you in whatever ways you need."

Notice how you can begin to love it again and notice how love is the first step to healing.

Our thoughts are of our own creation. They are not ultimate truth or the only reality. They are built within us based on our past experiences, our beliefs, our culture, our social and economic status, our family, and many other factors that build our own individual worlds. **There is nothing permanent or concrete**

about our thoughts. They can shift and change with the changes in our world, and we can rebuild them if they don't serve us.

As we begin to notice our thoughts and the reaction they create within us, we ask ourselves, "Are these thoughts helping or harming?" If they are not helping, then we slowly begin to let them go by turning our attention to more positive ones. We do not ignore our situation or what we are going through; we just choose to see it in ways that keep us aligned with who we want to be and how we want to show up in the world. We create a story that empowers us and keeps us motivated to be the best version of ourselves.

This is really important when we are experiencing pain and illness. A negative attitude towards our experience can sink us into a depression that tells us this experience is ruining our lives and taking everything that we value away. It can take away our hope of improvement and keep us from seeing all of the ways we can still participate in life and contribute our gifts to the world.

I had a client whose husband suffered from chronic pain. She said that there were two sides of him. His true self who used to be joyful and pleasant and the pain side that was angry, aggressive, and depressed. She said that his pain was like a monster that took over his whole being and turned him into someone totally different. None of their old friends wanted to spend time with them anymore, and many of them often questioned why she stayed with him when he was so emotionally abusive to her. She replied that she was one of the only people who could see that it was the pain talking, not him; she still loved the man that was hidden under the pain. He never sought help to disengage from his pain story nor from the negative thoughts around his pain that slowly turned him into this monster that no one wanted to be around. He alienated himself from all the positive people in his life and abused the one person who stood by his side. This is because he lost sight of what really matters. He focused on his loss and his pain instead of on who he wanted to be in the world and how he wanted to show up for others. The longer he spent in this negative mindset, the more it took over his whole being and became his whole reality.

This is a very different story from the character Morrie in the book *Tuesdays with Morrie*. This was a true story about a man who lived with ALS and how he used the experience to contribute more healing and insight to the world. He was a professor who loved teaching and inspiring people. He was very active and loved to dance. When ALS took over his body, he slowly began to lose all use of his physical body while his mind stayed intact. His slow decline created new experiences of loss everyday. He would allow himself to have those difficult moments and express his deep sadness and grief, but then he would shift his focus back onto what he valued most in the world and what was most important to him, teaching and inspiring. He used his experience to teach others about what it means to live a full and meaningful life. He continued teaching until the day he died by sharing his experience with others and teaching the lessons he was learning about what is most important in life even when you lose everything you thought brought you happiness. He taught about love, connection, and learning.[1] If you need inspiration for your own healing journey, this would be a great book for you to read.

There is an old teaching that has been used in many different spiritual practices that tells of a broken vase. Some see a broken vase and all they see are the cracks and fissures and how it makes that vase imperfect and unusable. Others look at the vase, hold it up to the light, and notice how those cracks and imperfections are the only places that the light shines into to the dark center. Our cracks and imperfections can be the source of our greatest light.

We cannot always control our health, but we can control how we relate to it and how we choose to experience it. Yes, it is hard to be sick and injured. Yes, we will grieve our losses and struggle with our limitations. But we don't have to get stuck in them. We can choose to place our focus back on what really matters and the ways we can access it in spite of what our bodies are capable of doing. We can focus on what energies we are cultivating within that we can share back with the world. Focusing on these will help us to move through our experience of pain and illness more peacefully with purpose. We will talk more on this in the next section on the heart and spirit.

You can use the following exercises to begin to shift your thought patterns around your illness or pain so that you can start to see the light shining through the cracks.

3.3 EXERCISES ON CREATING A HEALTHY RELATIONSHIP WITH EXPERIENCE

Reconstructing the thought wheel

You can begin with a breathing exercise to become present and connected. You will then step into that open space behind thought so that you can observe your thoughts without becoming engaged with them.

Notice their ever-changing nature. Find comfort in their impermanence. Pay attention to what thoughts continue to arise for you around your pain and illness.

Notice how they almost always repeat themselves over and over and are generated from something you heard, witnessed, or thought before.

You can imagine this cycle of thought like the wheel of fortune. You spin it around and land on different thoughts, but most of the thoughts on the wheel stay the same. Begin to notice the nature of the thoughts on your wheel.

Do most of them cause positive or negative reactions within you?

You can pick one of your thoughts to focus on.

When did you begin thinking this way?

What perception of the world and your place in it is it generating?

What perception of self is this thought based in?

What perception of your pain or illness is this thought creating?

Does this thought create the reality that I want to live in?

Does this thought allow you to have the experience you would like to have?

Does it help you to see the light shining through the cracks?

If not, then begin to transform the thought. Ask yourself, how could I see this differently?

How do I want to see the world?

How do I want to see myself?

How do I want to see this situation?

How do I want to see my pain and illness?

What thought would create the reality I want to live in?

You can continue in this way for the other thoughts on your wheel of fortune, until when you spin the wheel, each thought that you could possibly land on is one that creates the world you want to live in.

Developing a healthy relationship with experience

You can begin with a breathing exercise to become present and connected. You will then step into that open space behind thought so that you can observe your thoughts without becoming engaged with them. Find comfort in the impermanence of all mind states. They manifest, present themselves, transform, and fade away—always changing.

This reminds you that you don't have to take any one thought or mind state too seriously. Imagine a current situation in your life that you are resisting or struggling with. Imagine your experience with pain and illness.

Notice your relationship to it. Listen to your thoughts about it. Listen to your thoughts about self, the other, and the world.

What reaction are these thoughts creating in you?

What are they doing to your body and your mind?

Who are you being when you have them?

Is this who you want to be?

What reality are you living in when you have these thoughts?

Is this the reality you want to live in?

Begin to loosen your grasp on these mindsets and thoughts. They don't have to be your reality. Feel your body soften. Feel your mind open.

How do you want to see this situation and the world?

How do you need to relate to your pain and illness so that you can be the person you want to be?

How do you need to relate to this situation so that you can live in the world you want to live in?

Create the thoughts that best serve you and continue to repeat them to yourself.

A mind at peace is much more able to hear the wisdom of the body and the heart and spirit. Peace in the mind is attained when we are able to observe our thoughts, understand their effect on our internal state, and let go of the ones that aren't serving us. Creating a positive mind space helps us to listen because it can be open, free of judgment, and ready to listen without projecting old stories, opinions, fears, and desires onto what we are hearing. Otherwise, we may dismiss the wisdom that we are hearing because it does not fit with our old belief or story or it threatens an image of self.

Peace in the mind is attained when we are able to observe our thoughts, understand their effect on our internal state, and let go of the ones that aren't serving us. Creating a positive mind space helps us to listen because it can be open, free of judgment, and ready to listen without projecting old stories, opinions, fears, and desires onto what we are hearing. Otherwise, we may dismiss the wisdom that we are hearing because it does not fit with our old belief or story or it threatens an image of self.

A peaceful mind sees beyond our own limitations of perspective and opens to new ways of seeing life and our reality. It is willing to be changed by what it hears. Without this willingness to change, we may be able to hear what our body needs to heal but will block it out because it makes us uncomfortable or threatens an opinion or stance that we identified ourselves with previously. This would keep us from making the changes in our lives necessary to heal.

This state of openness and willingness to change is achieved by admitting that our limited minds don't know all the answers. We understand that our perception is limited by our small scope of the world. How we see things is shaped by where we grew up, how we were raised, our education, our economic status, our race, our culture, our society, our gender, and all the other factors that create our unique individual experience. We don't know the whole truth and we never will. We know the truth that exists in our reality, not the truth that exists for the greater whole.

This world and all of life existed before our arrival and will exist long after we are gone. We are not the center of the system, but one small part of it. All of the wisdom that it holds is accessible to us if we listen deeply, but the answers don't come from our limited minds. They come from the wisdom of that which is greater. In order to hear them we have to humble ourselves to our limited perspectives and ask to receive the wisdom of the world. As we are listening, we may hear things that threaten our old beliefs and fill us with doubt and fear. This is where trust comes in. A peaceful mind trusts in something so much bigger than itself and knows that it can let go of control and surrender to that guiding force. We will go more into that in the next section on the heart and spirit.

To open your mind into a peaceful state of receiving, you must start by humbling yourself to your limited views, become willing to see beyond them, and be changed by what you hear.

3.4 EXERCISES ON DEVELOPING A FLEXIBLE MIND

Is this true?

You can begin with a breathing exercise and then step into that clear open space behind thought.

Begin to observe your thoughts.

Notice which thoughts are loudest for you today. Notice what thoughts you are having about your pain or illness.

Notice what reactions they are creating in you and what emotions are behind those reactions.

Now ask yourself, "Is this true?"

Continue this for a few minutes, consistently noticing thought and then asking, "Is this true?"

As you continue asking, you will notice that your belief in the thought gets weaker.

Who says it's true?

Where did you hear that belief for the first time?

What perspective of the world is that thought based on? Is that perspective true?

Slowly, we become more and more open and less attached to our thoughts and views.

Notice how this helps us to let go of the thoughts that no longer serve us. The ones that limit us into our fear around pain and illness. The ones that tell us that this experience is all bad. This doesn't have to be true.

Notice how freeing that is and how much peace it brings into your mind space. You don't have to believe these thoughts.

Widening Perspective

You can begin with a breathing exercise and then step into that clear open space behind thought.

Begin to notice your thoughts and beliefs around your pain and illness. You can imagine one of those beliefs written on a piece of paper in front of you.

Notice how when you hold it close to you, it becomes all that you can see. It becomes the lens through which you see the world and your experience.

Notice how with it in front of you, you cannot see what's actually around you.

Now hold that belief back and widen your perspective. Open your range of sight up further and further. You can imagine yourself in any natural setting that you would like: mountains, beach, or meadow.

Notice that the more you allow into your sight, the more you are able to see. Watch how everything within nature is constantly changing—coming and going, transforming, and adapting.

Notice how nature does not hold on to one state or one truth. She allows everything to continue flowing and adapting, dying away, and beginning anew.

Allow your beliefs to do the same. As your context gets larger and larger, begin to imagine other social groups outside of your own.

Ask how do they see this pain or illness?

Then imagine other cultures and countries and ask, how do they see this pain or illness? Then step back and take the perspective of Mother Earth looking down on all of us and ask, how does she see this pain or illness?

Take your perspective even wider, out in space into the whole universe and ask, how does the cosmos see this pain and illness?

Now your own belief does not seem so big and important. Maybe it no longer seems true at all. Maybe you see that there is a truth so much bigger than the one you are living, and maybe that greater truth sees a greater purpose for the experience of pain and illness you are having. Maybe this is just one small part of your story that will manifest into something much bigger.

Notice how this fills your mind space with peace and acceptance.

4

Settling our emotions

Emotions always need to be addressed on our healing journeys. They can be at the root of our physical ailments and are
greatly affected by our physical ailments. We cannot separate
the two. Many people have done extensive research on how our
emotional world shows up in our physical one. Louise Haye has
many great books on the topic helping you to understand what
emotions or beliefs might be behind your physical experience.
Dr. Sarno was a medical doctor who realized that he couldn't
explain many of the pains his patients were experiencing without considering their emotional history. He based his practice
on psychosomatic pain, on the body's desire to cover up emotional trauma with physical pain. There has also been extensive
research on the physiological effects of emotions on the body.
We know that emotions change which hormones, enzymes, and

neurotransmitters are released within the body, changing our physiological systems.

When we feel fear, adrenaline is released in our system and we go into our fight, flight, or freeze mode. Our pupils dilate, our heart rate goes up, our breathing shallows, our blood moves away from our organs to our muscles, and our replenishing, recuperating, and rejuvenating systems get turned off. If our emotional world is unsettled, we may spend more time than necessary in this draining state, leading to physical ailments.

When we engage in reward-based activities like eating, sexual intercourse, and exercising, endorphins are released. Endorphins help us manage pain and discomfort. When we feel loved and cared for, we release oxytocin which helps us to feel calm and peaceful. Dopamine is released in reward-based activities and supports our motor function and memory. When we feel happy and positive, our serotonin levels are balanced, and serotonin helps us to digest food, sleep, heal wounds, strengthen bones, and possess a healthy sex drive.

These hormones work in coordination with our emotional world. Our perception of the world can cause thoughts and beliefs that bring up negative emotions; this can change which hormones are released within us, altering the functioning of our body. Illness and pain can make it harder for us to engage in the activities that bring us joy and reward-based satisfaction. This can decrease our emotional well-being which then makes it harder for us to heal because it turns off the hormones in charge of our rest, replenish, and rejuvenate systems. When we aren't feeling well, we lose motivation to engage in the activities and social connections that increase our emotional well-being, decreasing our mood even more and once again turning off the healing systems in our body. We can then lose motivation to engage in the practices and treatments that support our physical body, and this makes healing a slow and painful process.

We may also have chemical imbalances within us that alter our moods which in turn will continue the imbalance in our hormone release. It's the chicken-and-egg scenario and the medical system is still experimenting with how to regulate it all. Some doctors focus more on the physiological side and go right to drugs to fix the chemical imbalance while others focus more on healing the emotional and mental world in order to bring balance back to the physiological one. Again, I don't believe there is a right answer here. The only truth is that the emotional world is inseparable from the physical world, and both need to be healed together.

A variety of beliefs also exist related to the storage of past emotional traumas within the body, which manifest as physical ailments. Some practitioners feel that past traumas can be stored in our cells and muscles, altering cell growth and motor function. This could also be linked to the fear response certain situations trigger within us; these situations might possess similarities to past traumatic events and the body releases adrenaline causing our muscles to tighten and our cell regeneration to turn off. These physical changes within the body could also be linked to how we hold ourselves muscularly because of our emotional state. We may stand hunched over for years because of past abuse. We may constantly carry tension in our back muscles due to perceived lack of safety. We may have muscles that don't want to activate based on a fear around certain movements.

Our emotional trauma may also cause us to treat our bodies differently. Maybe we are really hard on our body, always pushing it to extremes because we want to feel those surges of adrenaline and endorphins that we don't get otherwise. We might force our body to stay up through the night and keep working through fatigue because we are stressed and anxious. Maybe our sadness and depression is decreasing our motivation so we become inactive and lethargic. All these changes will cause rippling effects within our physical body and could lead to illness and injury.

We can see that taking care of our emotional world is essential while trying to heal our physical one. When our emotional world is healthy and balanced, we treat our bodies better. While healing from illness or injury, a positive emotional state motivates us to engage in the activities and practices that will support the physiological systems that help us heal quicker.

In order to heal our emotional world, we have to be aware of what is going on within it. Many of us turn away from our emotions because we are afraid to feel them. We are under the impression that they will overwhelm us, creating negative consequences in our lives. This is not true. Emotions are simply energy pulsing through the body, we are the ones who create the reactions from that energy. If we simply observe the feelings within our body and mind without reacting to them, we can be with them without letting them dictate our behavior. We aren't afraid of the emotion; we are afraid of how it manifests in our words, actions, and thoughts.

We can begin by giving our emotions permission to be present. In our busy days we are told that our emotions don't belong, that they will get in the way of our productivity. So we push them aside or hide them away, but suppressed emotions don't just go away. They get stored within us and continue to build until one day we explode at something seemingly trivial because our emotions weren't getting the attention they needed. We need to make a safe time and space where we can address these emotions and listen to them. This isn't a time to tell the story of why we feel the way we do, blaming the world, our illness, or others for the emotions. This is a time to simply feel how the energy of the emotion shows up in our body and our mind.

Fear of our emotions goes away when we let go of the need to react to them, fix them, or force them to go away. When we simply sit with them in acceptance, their presence no longer disturbs us. We don't judge ourselves for having them because we know they are a natural part of life that everyone experiences. We cannot eliminate emotions, so why fight so hard to make them go away? Just feel. We allow ourselves to feel. We allow ourselves to be with our emotions in peace.

In order to create a safe space and time to listen to our emotions we need to remember what resources we have to take care of the difficult ones. We have to remember where our foundation lies and what keeps us centered and grounded. These may be external supports or they may be states of being that we know we can bring ourselves back to with our practices of self-care and self-love. When you feel an instability within you, what brings you back to center? What helps you to feel calm and grounded? Sometimes it's simply remembering who you are at your core and what you value most. We remember that we are love, peace, compassion, acceptance, and gratitude. We remember that we can return to that version of ourselves at any time by pausing, breathing, and settling. We remember that no matter how intense our emotions are, they are temporary manifestations of energy within us and they will eventually transform.

We also trust that just because we are present for our emotions it doesn't mean we have to act out of them. We can choose to feel the emotion without the emotion generating our words and actions. Anger does not have to be displayed with aggressive outbursts and yelling. Sadness does not have to seclude us and keep us from expressing our beauty. We can choose what to do with these emotional energies within us, and it can look very different from how we have expressed them in the past.

You can practice this now with the following exercises.

4.1 EXERCISES ON INVITING YOUR EMOTIONS INTO YOUR HEART SPACE

Creating a safe space

You can begin with a breathing exercise and then follow your breath into your heart space.

Feel the true nature of your heart space. It is open, loving, compassionate, and kind. In the heart space, there is room for all things. All things belong, even difficult emotions.

Recognize how this heart space is rooted in the foundation of your being and that, when connected with these roots, you are grounded enough to handle all things. Remember the supports you have developed for yourself. Remember how you engage in self-care and self-love.

You may even imagine the heart space and all of your self-care techniques as a kind and caring companion who can be present for the suffering part of you. Allow this strong and stable side of you to give you the courage to be vulnerable with this emotion.

Allow your heart space to grow wider and wider, opening in non-judgmental awareness.

Do you feel safe feeling your emotion here? Could you be present for your emotion without having to explain it, fix it, solve it, or force it to change?

Are there any fears present within you around feeling this emotion? That you will be overwhelmed, or judged, or that you will react in destructive ways?

Return to your heart again. Remember who you truly are: peace, love, compassion, acceptance, and gratitude. Remember that you have all the tools and supports necessary to be with this emotion in this peaceful moment. No need to fight it, just feel.

Can you invite your emotion in? Tell your emotion that you are here for it, that it is welcome in this space, that you want to be present for it.

Invite your emotion into this safe space you have created and simply be in its presence. It's OK to feel.

Letting go of old reactions

You can begin with a breathing exercise and then follow your breath into your heart space.

Invite your emotion into your heart space and be present for it.

Recall a time when you felt this emotion but forced it away. Examine your reaction to this emotion.

Why did you react the way you did?

What were you afraid of?

What do you think feeling that emotion will do to you?

What will feeling result in?

How has that emotion manifested in your words and your actions in the past?

Does it have to manifest that way?

Notice your relationship to that emotion.

Has feeling that emotion led to undesired outcomes before?

What were those outcomes?

Did the emotion have to lead to them?

Return to your heart space and hold the emotion here. Imagine yourself feeling that emotion in a healthy grounded state. How do you react?

What do you say and do?

Imagine yourself remaining calm and peaceful even in the presence of that emotion. Notice what relationship you have to that emotion now. Now are you afraid of that emotion?

In this safe space that we've created, we begin to observe the emotions present in our lives at this moment. When we are going through illness and injury, there will be many emotions involved in the experience. These emotions will change in each moment and will develop new complexities with each new leg of our healing journey. We aren't trying to get to any one emotional state, we are simply observing the one we are in.

When we are in pain or aren't feeling well, the physical sensations can take all of our attention and we forget to address our emotional experience. The physical sensations are creating emotional reactions within us that cause us to behave differently, and we can start believing that this is who we really are. We really are this grumpy, depressed, unmotivated person. This is not true. This is the expression of the emotions caused by our illness or injury. It is not our whole being. There is still another side of us that is happy, loving, and motivated. **Recognizing the emotions that are causing our negative behavior can help us to distance ourselves from them and remember that we are much more than this one experience. We are much more than the emotional state brought on by our illness.**

Feeling our emotions is what helps us to understand what is going on within us and why we are behaving the way we are. We can recognize the emotion and then simply observe the way it shows up in our body, in our thoughts and perceptions, and in our words and actions. Each emotion turns us into a different version of ourselves and reflects different needs that we have. In order to come back to who we truly are, our loving, compassionate, peaceful selves, we have to listen to these emotions and honor their needs.

Often times when I'm in a lot of pain, my temper is short and I become irritated easily. If I stop and observe my feelings in those moments, I notice that I am feeling vulnerable and scared. Fear often leads to aggressive behavior because we are trying to protect ourselves from harm. When I notice the fear behind the irritation, I'm more compassionate with myself and recognize that I probably just need a little bit more TLC in order to return to my loving kind self.

We can start by remembering that we are much more than this one experience. We remember who we are when we are at our best, when we are feeling grounded and centered and stable. This is the version of ourselves that best serves us and the world around us. As this person, we can live out our true values. We recognize that we can still be this person, even through our illness or injury, if we simply nurture ourselves and meet the emotional needs that we have.

Once we remember the truest version of ourselves, we can begin to observe our emotional state in this moment. We don't judge or try to change, we just observe. We recognize how it shows up in our body, in our thoughts and perceptions, and in our words and actions. This helps us to understand who this emotion turns us into and what experience of the world it generates. We recognize that this is the experience of this one emotion; it is not the whole truth. There is a different way for us to see the world and experience it that reflects our true selves, our grounded, centered, and stable selves. For now, we just remember the possibility as we observe our current emotional state.

4.2 EXERCISES ON OBSERVING YOUR EMOTIONS

Remembering your true self

Come back home to the breath and follow it into your heart. Use the wisdom of the heart to observe who you truly are. Imagine a time when you felt truly grounded, centered, and stable. A time when you felt good about your body, your mind felt settled, and your spirit felt true. Notice who you were being in that moment.

How does your body feel?

What are your energy levels?

What is your posture?

What is your facial expression?

What are you telling yourself about the world, other people, and yourself? Who are you being?

When you are fully nurtured, what are you expecting from the world and others?

What are you receiving from the world and your loved ones?

What is your relationship to the world and your friends and family?

What are you offering the world and humankind and how are they receiving it?

What is your purpose?

Feel this best version of yourself in your heart and core.

Know that being this person is always a possibility if you consistently nurture yourself and look to the right sources for all your fundamental needs.

Identifying your emotions

You can begin with a breathing exercise and then step into that open space behind thought. Remember that the emotions you feel right now are only one experience. Remember that the true version of yourself is always available to you even though you are going through this emotional experience at this moment.

As you begin to observe your thoughts begin to notice if there are emotions associated with the thoughts. Name the emotion that you find.

Now switch your attention to your body and begin to feel all the ways in which this emotion manifests within your body.

Where do you tighten?

Where does your energy go?

What hurts?

Do any muscles weaken?

What is your posture?

What is your heart feeling?

What are your hands doing?

What is your facial expression?

Now come back to the mind and notice how this emotion is affecting your thoughts.

What are you thinking about self?

What are you thinking about the other and the world?

What perspective do you have about the world?

Is this the only true perspective?

How do you interact with the world when you are having this emotion?

Who are you being?

You can continue this exercise by scanning through your day and noticing other times during the day that this emotion was present. Notice how it changed who you were being.

You can also use this meditation throughout the day, becoming aware of when this emotion is present and catching it in the moment. Do this exercise many times to become aware of all the different emotions present within you. You will be surprised to realize that they are always present and they are always affecting who you are being.

Now that we are aware of our emotions and who they turn us into, we can start listening to their needs. When we are ill or injured, we have different emotional needs than we normally do, and these needs can change rapidly. Our emotional needs always boil down to our most basic human needs: love, acceptance, belonging, safety, nourishment, and stability. We usually need a lot more love, acceptance, and belonging when we are ill or injured because we can feel alienated from our usual forms of socializing and connecting with the world around us. We also need more support and safety because we feel extra vulnerable and scared. Recognizing these needs helps us to ask for support and engage with the practices that meet these needs.

As we are listening to our emotional needs, we have to listen under the initial story. When we first get emotionally triggered, we want to blame the experience on what happened in our external world. We may blame the doctor for being short with us. We may blame our spouse for not listening when we needed to tell our story. We may blame a friend for canceling our lunch date at the last minute. These are stories around why you felt an emotion, and they cause us to believe the solution lies in controlling other people and getting them to do what we want. The doctor should learn better bedside manner. Our spouse should learn how to listen. Our friend should learn common courtesy. Placing the blame and solution outside of ourselves only makes us feel more vulnerable and upset, because most of the time we cannot control what other people do or say.

This usually results in us reacting in ways that actually make it harder for us to get our need met. We yell at the doctor and now he doesn't want to spend more time with us. We sulk off, avoiding our spouse for the rest of the evening, and don't get the acceptance we were looking for. We cold-shoulder our friend and don't get the connection we needed. Observing the actual need behind the emotion, instead of just telling the story of why we feel that way, helps us to understand how to respond in ways that get us closer to the outcome we wanted.

Observing the true need of the emotion empowers us to take care of our own internal state. It recognizes that this external thing that happened to us did not cause the emotion, it simply triggered a vulnerability or insecurity that we already had and weren't taking care of. Our society has told us that feeling a need for belonging and acceptance and that asking for help is weak. Quite the opposite is true. As Brene Brown says, "Vulnerability is not weakness. I define vulnerability as emotional risk, exposure, uncertainty. Vulnerability sounds like truth and feels like courage. Truth and courage aren't always comfortable, but they're never weakness."[2]

There is nothing more difficult than being vulnerable enough to admit our true needs when we have been hurt. It is much easier to give the cold shoulder or stand in self-righteous anger than to admit that our heart was deeply hurt because our need for acceptance was threatened. Admitting our true needs takes serious courage. It even takes courage to admit our needs to ourselves. Sometimes we don't want to look at the true reason we're sad because we're scared that we won't be able to meet the causal need we uncover. It's easier to keep fighting with our spouse than to admit that what we really need is to feel like we belong. Belonging feels like a hard thing to attain, but trying to control our spouse with anger definitely won't get us any closer.

Even though it is difficult to admit our true needs, we have to do it if we want to heal. We can do this by letting go of the story about why the external world made us feel this emotion and listening to what felt threatened or vulnerable within us.

Illness and injury heighten our vulnerabilities, in turn creating strong emotional states. Instead of blaming the illness for our emotions, we can look at what basic need within ourselves felt threatened by the illness.

For example, when my back was at its worst and I couldn't do any of my usual activities, I felt frustrated and sad most of the time. I could have simply blamed the emotion on the injury and tried to distract myself or push it away. Instead I turned inward and asked, "What really feels threatened here?" For me, it was my need for connection. I thought that if I was unable to go skiing and biking that my friends wouldn't want to spend time with me, because those were the activities we usually did together. Now I understand my sadness better and could respond in a way that would help meet my true need. I could reach out to my friends and share my sadness and ask to schedule time with them that didn't involve high-impact sports. This would help me to move through my sadness towards healing.

You can use the following exercises to look beyond your pain or illness story to the real root of your emotional experience.

4.3 EXERCISES ON OBSERVING THE NATURE OF EMOTIONS

Recognizing the story behind your emotion

You can begin with the previous exercise on naming your emotion and then inviting it into your heart space.

Once your emotion is present within your heart space being held and supported, you can begin to investigate the story behind it.

Are you blaming your emotion on your illness or injury?

Are you blaming the situation you are in because of your illness or injury?

What about your physical experience or current situation is so hard?

What are you telling yourself is causing this emotion?

Are you desperately needing something to be different or fixed?

Are you resisting something or clinging to something?

What perspective do you have of self, the other, and the world?

Is this true?

Are you reacting to your current experience or out of its resemblance to a previous experience?

Are you making predictions for how things will be in the future and reacting to that prediction?

Now, look around you. Come back to the present moment. Silence the story.

What's really happening?

Are you safe?

Are you OK?

Is there any immediate threat?

Do you need to remain in this emotional state?

Settle back into your breath and the present moment, allowing the emotion to soften. You may want to repeat to yourself that in this moment, you are okay and safe. For just this moment, you can breathe and be still. For just this moment, you don't have to fix anything or solve it. You can just be with the emotion and the experience in peace, letting go of the story about why you're feeling this way and simply feeling.

Listening to what the emotion is really telling you

This exercise can be done after the previous one. Once you have allowed your emotion to be present and then soften, you can begin to investigate what the emotion was trying to tell you. Normally our emotions are trying to keep us safe or alert us to one of our basic needs that felt threatened or vulnerable.

What was it that made you unsettled?

Was it alerting you to a potential danger?

Did you feel like you were losing something? What was it?

Were you afraid of what would happen in the future? What and why?

What feels vulnerable right now?

Is there one of your basic needs that feels threatened?

Maybe the need for belonging, connection, love, acceptance, safety, stability, or nourishment?

Now that you understand why the emotion arose, it shouldn't have the same urgency. Allow the emotion to soften as you settle into the understanding of your actual situation. Notice the reaction that you usually have to the emotion.

Does this reaction get you closer to what you were really wanting?

Does the reaction help or harm you?

What response would actually move you closer to your desired outcome? Imagine yourself responding in this way. How does it feel?

What response do you get from the world and the others?

Did it move you closer to who you want to be and the outcome you wanted to experience?

Now that we understand the true need behind our emotions, we can nurture them. This takes more creativity when we are ill or injured, because most likely we can't participate in our usual social activities or self-care practices. When I'm feeling lonely, I usually call someone to go for a hike or a bike ride. When I'm feeling self-doubt, I usually find a very doable household chore to tackle so that I get the satisfaction of completing something. When I feel unsettled, I usually do my yoga practice to reunite my mind and body in peace. All of these self-care techniques are very difficult when my body is unwell. So I have to be more creative in how to meet them. When illness and injury have drained us of our motivation and energy, this can seem really difficult. It may require asking a loved one for support—share what feels vulnerable and what need you have, and ask for help knowing how to address it.

There are many different ways to meet our basic needs. We tend to adopt a few and only engage in those. Then, when we are no longer able to do those activities, we feel like we have lost all of our means for staying emotionally well. Instead of focusing on the self-care practices that we are no longer able to do, we can focus on the need that they were meeting and ask ourselves, "How else could I meet this need?" If the need is connection and your usual way of getting it is to play soccer, you may feel a huge loss when you break your leg and can't play. But connection comes in many other forms. You could play a board game instead, or have a dinner party, or go for tea.

As we make these shifts in our lives, we will feel grief over losing our favorite forms of self-care. Hopefully, for many of us the loss will only be temporary, and we will be able to return to them once we are healed. Sometimes the change is more permanent, and we will go through a long period of denial, anger, sadness, and ideally acceptance before we are able to thrive with our new forms of self-care. These forced changes can be an amazing opportunity for self-discovery and expansion.

When I am healthy, I spend most of my time outdoors recreating. It was only when illness forced me to stop that I was able to discover my love for painting, music, and writing. I suppose I always had an interest in them, but I let my active side dominate, never giving the artist an opportunity to grow. Sickness was what slowed me down enough to do so. Frida Kahlo and many other famous artists suffered from tremendous physical limitations that gave them the time and motivation to express themselves through art. Yes, we will grieve our lack of ability to do our "preferred" self-care practices, but through forced change some of us may discover hidden passions that we never allowed to grow.

If we are grieving some of our lost self-care practices or activities, we can look at the need we felt they were meeting. Some may have been meeting several: connection, belonging, a sense of worth. Then we can begin to explore other ways of getting those needs met. We may not find one activity that meets all of the same needs at once, so we may need to divide them between several. It may feel challenging to motivate ourselves to engage in these new activities, but as time goes on and we start feeling the happiness they bring, it will become easier and easier. This is how we nurture our emotions back into peace.

You can use the following exercise to identify how to nurture your emotional needs.

4.4 EXERCISE ON NURTURING YOUR EMOTIONS

Nurture your emotions

You can begin with the exercise of listening to your emotion's true needs. Arrive at the root cause of the emotion.

Was it a cry for safety, love, acceptance, or belonging?

Examine where you were looking to meet this need.

Was it a healthy, sustainable way of meeting the need?

Is this means of meeting the need available to you now?

If your illness or injury is preventing you from engaging in this self-care practice, notice how that compounds your emotional experience.

What feeling does that bring up for you?

What need feels like it cannot be met because you are unable to do this activity?

Can you open yourself to the possibility of meeting this need in a different way?

You can grieve the loss of your previous ways of meeting this need while remaining open to discovering new ways. Try to remember the sources of support and nourishment that come from within your own heart.

Enter your own heart space. Connect with that truth within you. Recognize how you are connected to all things.

Know that this source of love and safety and belonging resides within you.

Know that when you accept yourself, you always belong. When you love yourself, you are always loved. When you accept your place in the greater system, you always find safety within it.

Find your source of these needs. You can say this out loud or to yourself, "I am here for you. You are loved. You are accepted just as you are. You are safe. Everything belongs within the greater system."

Offer yourself anything else that your emotion is asking for. Rest in this place of peace and acceptance.

5

Settling the heart and spirit

Pain and illness can wreak havoc in our spiritual world or they can strengthen it greatly. Sometimes, if pain and illness continue to affect us over and over, we can lose faith in that greater force that we believed in. We may curse it, asking why this is happening to us and why it wants to spite us. This then makes us feel even lonelier and more afraid because we have lost faith in the one constant support that is always there for us. This doesn't have to happen.

We can choose to use our experience of pain and illness to increase our spiritual practice. It can be a motivator to dive deeper and learn more. If we have something that gives us purpose and meaning, we are better able to face whatever comes and transform it into growth.

This was the purpose of Viktor Frankl's work as a psychologist. After surviving the death camps of WWII and losing every member of his family except for one sister, he chose to use the experience as an opportunity to understand the human experience better and learn what it was that helped people not only survive these atrocious events but grow from them. He found that having a sense of purpose and meaning is what helped them emerge from the unimaginable with hope and motivation to move forward. He says in his book *Man's Search for Meaning,* "Those who have a 'why' to live, can bear with almost any 'how'." [4]

I call this our big "why." The "why" that becomes the motivation, intention, and foundation behind our every action, word, and thought. Having a spiritual practice can help us define this "why" and, in fact, our big "why" can be our spiritual practice. For example, my big "why" is to be a source of compassion and peace for the world. I don't have a specific religion that I identify with, but I do try to live in a way that constantly supports and cultivates more compassion and peace within me. This helps me to look at every experience as a new opportunity to learn more about myself and my limitations around my big "why." I use that understanding to shift the patterns or beliefs within me that prevent me from being compassionate and peaceful in any particular situation. This gives meaning to everything that I go through. Even the really hard times I spend living through pain and illness can help me build more compassion and peace.

When we are first developing our big "why," we have to widen our thinking beyond the dogma and ritual of our religion. This is deeper than doctrine. This is why we are supposedly following the doctrine. It's what the doctrine is supposed to be doing for us: creating more love, peace, compassion, and acceptance in our world. Many of us get so focused on the doctrine that we start acting, speaking, and thinking in ways that don't actually align with the purpose and meaning behind it. We start judging others and trying to convert them instead of focusing on being compassionate towards them and building more acceptance and love in our world. We may also start condemning and judging ourselves—blaming ourselves for what is going wrong in our lives, because we haven't been complying with all our religious guidelines. This does not help us to heal. It creates more stress within our being, which we have already learned impedes healing.

Our first step is to break away from the dogmatic views we have been holding and return to what really matters. We notice what clinging to our beliefs does to our internal state and to how we treat ourselves and others. We look into how our beliefs change the way we approach healing. We notice if they are limiting us in our means of getting support and care or telling us that we can't seek medical advice from certain people or we can't engage in certain procedures or practices. We notice the effect this is having on our well-being. Is it actually serving our health in the best way possible?

This is a very tricky topic and, like everything else, will be specific to each person. I once taught at a Christian Science school and was the only non-Christian Scientist working there. I knew nothing about their beliefs before starting and learned a lot through observation. There were many things that I loved about their lifestyle choices and how they approached their spirituality. I began to observe the way they viewed healthcare and learned that they did not believe in using any form of Western medicine. They would not consume any type of mind-altering substance, including medications. Every illness was a manifestation of the mind and spirit and could be cured in that realm.

They had Christian Science practitioners who would treat the ill with prayer and spiritual guidance. They truly believed that the body could heal itself if it was given enough spiritual support. I could see how this approach could serve them in many ways; and for day to day aches and pains, it probably did keep them healthier to try to remedy those things through more natural means. I could also see how it empowered them to believe in the ability of their spirituality to cure them, a faith that created a helpful guide in their lives. However, once the clinging to the belief became too extreme, I saw individuals struggling with problems years after the inciting incidents that could easily have been fixed with casts or surgeries. They were still walking limps limited in everything they did, because of injuries that never got the medical attention they needed. One could say that this was a part of the larger plan for them and motivated them to now live in a way that permitted them to serve others how they were meant to. But it all depends on what each individual values most and what being "healed" means to them.

I say this not to judge others' choices, but to open up your mind to exploring all the ways our beliefs can affect the choices we make regarding our health. There is truth in the body's ability to heal itself. I imagine most of us have witnessed that. This is not far from what many of the alternative healers that I went to for the ruptured disc in my back believed, and I myself was drawn to it when Western medicine failed to produce a good cure for my pain. But, when the body is struggling to heal itself, it may be beneficial to reach out to the support that's available. If our beliefs tell us that this is wrong, we may want to take a second look at those beliefs and ask if they are really there to serve us in the best way possible.

You can begin to expand beyond your own views by exploring how they influence the choices you make around your healing and how they affect the way you treat yourself and others.

5.1 EXERCISE ON OPENING TO SPIRITUAL DIFFERENCE

You can begin with a breathing exercise and then open the mind. Once you have become the observer rather than the thinker, you can begin to examine the beliefs that you cling to.

When did you first hear that these beliefs were so important?

What did they do for you?

What are they doing for you now?

Notice how your need for these beliefs to be right affects who you are.

What does protecting these do to your interaction with others who have different views?

What does protecting these beliefs do to your ability to love and accept everyone?

Who do you become when you try to prove your beliefs?

What does clinging to these beliefs do to your relationship with yourself? Do you judge yourself? Do you condemn yourself?

What does this relationship with the world and yourself do to your ability to heal?

What perspective does it give you of your pain and illness?

Does it give you the grace to make new choices around your healing and engage in different practices that may serve you better?

What does it do to your ability to listen to your own body and ask it what it really needs?

Is this who you want to be? Is this a true representation of your spiritual self?

Open yourself beyond this belief. Admit that maybe we do not know the ultimate truth and maybe there is more to this truth than the beliefs we have been clinging to.

Rest in the comfort and ease of not having to cling to these beliefs. Trust yourself to be able to listen to what your own heart tells you about your health.

Feel the peace that it brings you.

Are you softer?

Are you better able to listen to your true needs?

Are you better able to live out your spirituality in a non-judgmental and loving way?

Can you give yourself the grace to heal fully even if it looks different from what you believed was right before?

Once we are open to exploring beyond our own beliefs, we can come back to what we truly value most. This is what is at the center of our being, the core of our true happiness—what we really want to experience in life. This is what we are hoping that our religion, faith, or spiritual practice is actually giving us. It is a feeling, an energy, a state of being. I always come back to the core of what I believe true happiness and well-being is built on: love, peace, acceptance, compassion, and gratitude. If we cultivate these things within us and share them out with the world, then happiness and joy come to us with ease.

Where most of us go astray is when we believe external conditions will bring us these things. We think that in order to have them we have to be healthy, wealthy, powerful, successful, married, parents, or any other external condition that might bring us into a state of happiness. Seeking these things, believing that they will bring us peace, actually takes us further away from what we truly value. We start to obsess over our status and what we have, hoping once we arrive at this perfect image of happiness, we will actually feel it, but we never do. We are chasing a false idol of happiness.

So we switch our focus: not to the conditions we believe will make us happy in the future but the conditions of happiness are present for us here and now. Even if we are ill and in pain. Even if we don't have that perfect job. Even if we haven't gotten married yet. How can we cultivate those feelings of love, compassion, acceptance, peace, and gratitude right here and right now? And then we build towards our future on a foundation of these energies, and we carry them into whatever manifests in our lives, even if it's not the perfect image we hold for ourselves.

When we are in pain or struggling with illness, it can be hard to see what is going well in our lives. It is a part of our survival strategy to keep our awareness on our weak and vulnerable places so that we don't hurt them more. Pain very naturally draws our attention to it, because that is its job. It is there to remind us not to do the things that might cause more damage to our injured part. Illness is meant to hold our attention so that we are motivated to rest and nurture it. The problem is when we forget to look at what is still going well and what remains beautiful in our lives. We sink into a depression. This depression keeps us from engaging in the positive mindsets and habits that will help us heal. Therefore, we want to continue our cultivation of gratitude even when our physical form is struggling.

We can start by refocusing on our gratitude for all the miracles of life and conditions of happiness present for us in this moment. Even if we aren't feeling well or our bodies are limited, we are still surrounded by many gifts. We switch our attention to those gifts, and we allow ourselves to feel the happiness that they bring us. These could be as simple as a roof over our head, our dog who cuddles with us, the food on our table, the beautiful flower opening in our garden. We can also focus on all the miraculous things our body is still able to do for us—all that it is doing in each and every moment to keep us alive in spite of this illness or injury that we are living. Even if we can't feel the joy from these things right away, keep placing our attention on them giving them time to gain our appreciation.

Once we are more focused on the positive energies in our lives, we can remember what our heart and spirit value most. We will most likely find that what our body is capable of doing doesn't have as much to do with what really matters as we first thought. Even if our body is struggling, we can still feel and receive love. We can still develop compassion for ourselves and others. We can still cultivate more peace inside of ourselves and share it with the world. We can do these things no matter what state our body is in. Recognizing this brings us more acceptance for what our body is going through and inspiration for how we can have purpose and meaning even if our body is imperfect.

You can begin to find your heart's true values with the following exercises.

5.2 RECONNECTING WITH YOUR HEART'S VALUES

Becoming aware of the miracles of life

You can begin with a breathing and centering exercise. Turn back inward, reconnecting with self.

Open beyond your stories, opinions, and judgments. Begin to experience in open-minded awareness.

Look into where you are right here and right now. Notice all the little miracles that you normally overlook. Notice the roof over your head. Notice the food in your fridge. Notice that you have running water. Notice that you have a warm shower. Notice that you have shoes to wear. Notice that you have clothes to wear. Notice that you have a car to drive. Notice everything that is present in your life that makes everyday living comfortable and convenient for you. Allow these things to bring you joy.

Now look into the people in your life. Notice your loved ones. Notice how they show up for you. Notice your pets and the love they bring you. Notice the people who serve you in your town: the grocery store clerk, your waitress, the barista, the police, the DJs, the gas station attendants, and all the other people who show up to serve you everyday. Notice your friends and all that they do for you. Allow these people to bring you joy.

Now look into all the things that you are capable of. Look at what you can still do even though you may be sick or injured. Notice what your body is still doing to keep you alive and well. Notice how you are still here, able to experience this miraculous gift of life. Acknowledge the gifts and talents that you have. Acknowledge the ways you contribute to your community or your family. Acknowledge that you still have purpose and meaning even if your body is imperfect. Allow that to fill you with a sense of joy.

Remember in gratitude all the little miracles of life always present for you, and allow that to bring you a sense of happiness and peace.

Listening to the heart

This exercise is best done after completing exercises 4.1 so that you are able to see past the limitations of imposed beliefs. Once you are open and present, focus your attention inward on your heart center.

Feel the heart expanding and contracting with each breath. Allow the heart to open to the world on the inhalation and then re-center on your heart's values on the exhalation. Open at the same time as centering on the heart's truth. You can begin to listen to the heart.

What does the heart value most?

How does the heart want to interact with the world?

What does the heart want to offer the world?

What really matters to the heart?

How does the heart see you, the world, and others?

Who are you being when you are living from the heart?

Where does your grounding and foundation come from?

What does it feel like to live from the heart?

Does the heart feel limited by your illness or injury or can it live its purpose here, too?

Sit in this feeling and observe how it feels to be in the world when grounded in the heart. See who you are being. See what you are offering. Observe what you say and how others receive your words.

See yourself living from the heart even when your body is imperfect.

3

Learning to Listen and Honor What We Hear

6

Listening to the Body

Once we are settled and peaceful within the body, mind, and spirit, we can begin listening to understand what our true needs are. We begin with listening to the body. The body wants to heal, and it knows what it needs in order to do so. We just have to listen to it. Every experience within the body is telling us to move towards certain behaviors, thoughts, and connections and to move away from others. Pain is the body's defense mechanism, warning us not to do certain movements that may harm us more. Illness is the body's way of expelling a foreign unwanted intruder in our system. True healing means that we don't just treat the symptom, we understand the root cause the body is trying to warn us about.

We want to create a safe environment and lifestyle for our body so that it doesn't feel like it needs to protect itself from certain movements. We want to create a balanced and supportive environment within our bodies so that they don't feel like they have to defend themselves against toxins and waste. Yet most of us resist the changes that the body is asking us to make.

There are many ways that we distract ourselves from the wisdom of our bodies. This may be because we are afraid of the changes the body will ask us to make, or we are afraid of the consequences of the pain that we feel, or we are afraid of the lifestyle shift required during illness. We turn away from the body and ignore its message. This leads to an intensification of the body's defense, leading to more pain and more illness.

As Mark Nepo says, "To listen is to lean in softly with the willingness to be changed by what you hear."[8] When we listen to the body, we have to be willing to honor what it's asking us to do. I know all too well the difficulty of this. The pain in my back flares up whenever I am taking on too much and trying to carry every burden on my own. It also flares up whenever I am pushing too hard with my sports, trying to keep up with everyone else to prove that I am capable. I can feel the warning signs when it is getting ready to flare up, and yet many times I fail to listen. I fail to listen because I don't want it to be true. I want to be able to carry everything on my own because asking for help and trusting other people is hard for me. I want to be able to ski as hard as everyone else because I'm afraid they won't want to ski with me if I can't, and I don't want to lose those moments of connection. These fears keep me from listening, and the consequence is three months of not being able to lift more than five pounds, bend, or twist. Is it worth it?

In order to truly listen to the body, we have to be willing to honor what we hear. Many of us ask to be better, we say we want to be healed, but when our body tells us to change our lifestyle, we can't actually do it. The first time I went through my back injury, I was stuck in pain for three years. A healer once asked me if I actually wanted to heal, and I laughed at her saying, "Of course I want to heal. Who wouldn't want to end this pain?" She looked at me and said, "You aren't ready to heal yet." I was so angry with her. Who did she think she was telling me I didn't want to heal this debilitating injury. But she was right. I did want the pain to go away, but I didn't want to accept the lifestyle changes it was asking me to make. When I was asking to heal, I kept saying that I just wanted things to go back to the way they were. The problem was that how I was living my life was not supporting the well-being of my mind, body, and spirit. So my body waited to heal until I was willing to move forward in a new way aligned with true health.

We can start by asking ourselves if we are ready to listen to our bodies. This requires letting go of our image of what we should be able to do and accepting what the body is telling us it needs us to do. If we are clinging to false sources of happiness and well-being, then we may feel a resistance. We may imagine that we could never be happy unless we can continue eating gluten, or skiing double black diamonds, or drinking alcohol and staying out late. But if we recognize that true happiness comes from who we are being and what we are cultivating within, then we don't have to cling to these external conditions to be OK. We see that we can find happiness in every experience as long as we are able to cultivate love, compassion, peace, acceptance, and gratitude.

You can practice this with the following exercise.

6.1 EXERCISE ON BEING WILLING TO CHANGE

You can begin with a breathing and centering exercise. Return to your heart's center and what really matters to you. Remember that this has very little to do with what your body is able to do and much more to do with who you are being under any circumstance. Hold this in your awareness as you begin to explore your willingness to listen.

As you are asking to heal, are you making demands on your body for what you want it to be able to do?

Do you want to return to a lifestyle that pushes it beyond its healthy limits?

What are you asking the body to do: work long hours, carry all the burdens of your whole family, tackle taxing physical pursuits?

How does this feel in your body?

Does it tighten your muscles, increase your heart rate, and shallow your breathing?

Are you willing to let these demands go and listen to what the body really needs?

Look into what you are assuming will make you happy. Ask your body if this is what's best for it.

Is this the only way for you to be happy?

Is it worth compromising your health?

Are you willing to change in order to honor the needs of your body?

Tell your body that you are willing to change your lifestyle based on its needs. Repeat this over and over until you start to live it.

When we listen to the body, we can ask it what we do that makes it easier for it to show up as its best self and what we do that makes it more difficult. In order to do this we have to understand what the body feels like when it is at its best. This doesn't necessarily mean that it is out climbing Mount Everest and winning beauty contests. This means that it is at peace with itself, capable of loving itself, and capable of offering positivity to the world.

Sometimes, if we are climbing mount Everest and winning beauty contests, we are so absorbed in the expectations we put on our body that we cannot show up for others. This would not be the body at its best. A loving relationship with our body means that we appreciate what it is capable of without judging its limitations. We use its gifts, talents, and strengths to live with meaning and purpose. If we are constantly critiquing our body and pushing it to be more, then we build a negative relationship with ourselves which is reflected in how we treat others and the planet.

In order to define how our body is when it's at its best we have to remember what matters most to us, returning to our heart's values. Again, these have nothing to do with what we are capable of doing, they are in who we are being. We remember that when we are at our best we are able to cultivate love, compassion, peace, acceptance, and gratitude anywhere. We place ourselves in a situation when we felt capable of showing up in this way, and we observe how the body felt in that moment. Maybe we still had pain, but how were we relating to that pain? Maybe we were still ill, but how did we show up for that illness? We observe how it felt to be at peace with the body and what that did for our presence in the world.

You can practice this now with the following exercise.

6.2 THE BODY AT ITS BEST

You can begin with a breathing and centering exercise. Return to your heart's center and what really matters to you. Remember that this has very little to do with what your body is able to do and much more to do with who you are being. Remember what you value most and how you want to show up in the world.

Imagine a time when you were able to show up in this way for yourself, others, and the world. Picture where you were, who you were with, what you were doing and saying, and who you were being.

What did it feel like to be this version of yourself?

What did your body feel like in that moment?

Were you focused on what your body was accomplishing and what it was capable of doing, or were you focused on how it was showing up for others and who you were able to be in your body?

Did you feel at peace with your body?

Could you appreciate all the things that it was doing for you?

Could you see how it was serving you?

Did this ease your judgment and expectation of the body?

Were you still experiencing pain or illness in that moment?

How were you relating to that pain or illness?

Notice who you were able to be when your body was at peace, when you were capable of accepting and loving your body. Is this who you want to be in the world?

7

Listening to what the body knows about our mind

Now that we have a good idea of what our body feels like at its best, we can begin to explore what helps it stay in that state. We can begin with our thoughts and perceptions. We look at how we are relating to our bodies and what they are going through. Our thoughts and perceptions change the way we heal. If we are constantly thinking that our body is flawed and broken, then we will behave in ways that perpetuate that reality. Contrarily, if we believe that our body is capable of healing itself and that it is meant to be whole and healthy, it will return to that state.

There has been amazing research on the power of the mind to alter our bodies. People who have lost limbs and still feel excruciating pain show us that the mind can create sensations from what it believes to be true. Individuals have healed what was labeled as life-long paralysis by envisioning their spine reforming. Individuals who suffered from brain injuries that caused loss of motor function in the body, thought to be incurable, cured themselves by training the other side of the brain to take over.[3]

There is no limit to what the mind can do to help heal the body, but it requires training the mind to focus on thoughts and beliefs that serve us. This is easier said than done. We have been programmed to look outside of ourselves for healing and to trust everyone but ourselves when it comes to understanding our physical needs. Whenever we are ill, we are told to go to a doctor to find out what's wrong instead of listening to our own bodies. This creates a distrust between our mind and our body. There is a lack of communication between the two. We stop believing that the body knows what it needs to heal and that it is capable of doing so.

When we are given a diagnosis, the words of the doctor sit in our minds and hearts, creating a new reality for us. "Incurable" plays on repeat as we imagine the remainder of our lives being directed by this illness. We start believing this new narrative, and we get stuck in one image of ourselves: sick. We start living our lives in a way that reflects this narrative: going out less, limiting what we do, going to the doctor more often, and losing the other parts of our identity. Yes, we may be facing illness, but does this mindset serve us and our healing?

Instead we could look at the interpretation of the doctor and accept it as one way of seeing things. We don't have to discredit their diagnosis or treatment advice, but we don't have to passively acquiesce and lose our own voice. We ask ourselves how we want to see this experience and how we want to relate to it. Does it help us show up for life as our best selves when we believe we will never get better and that we have to be on drugs for the rest of our lives? Does it help us live as our best selves to believe that the body can't heal itself? This doesn't mean throw our treatments to the wayside and simply rely on the power of the mind. It means that we build a perception of our reality that helps us face the healing process with more hope, inspiration, and purpose.

We can look into our thoughts around our physical experience, from the way we talk to our bodies when we look in the mirror to how we relate to an experience of pain. We observe from a distance, not judging the thoughts we have or trying to push them away, simply watching and noticing the effect they have on our well-being. We notice that we are more than our thoughts and that we are able to alter them to serve us better. Each time we have a thought, we ask, "Does this help me to have a positive, healthy relationship with my body? Does this help me to live as my best self? Does this align with who I want to be in the world?" If the answer is no, then we let the thought go and redirect to a thought that is more helpful to us.

You can use the following exercise to listen to your thoughts about your body.

7.1 LISTENING TO YOUR THOUGHTS ABOUT THE BODY

You can begin with a breathing and centering exercise, then move into a body scan. Scan through all the parts of your body and, as you are connecting with the sensations in each body part, listen to what you think about it.

Do you speak kindly to this body part?

Do you believe that this body part is doing its best to keep you alive and well?

Is there judgment here?

Are you blaming this body part for your discomfort or difficulty?

Are you wishing this body part could be different or better?

Is there love in the way you are thinking about your body?

Are these thoughts helping you to heal and be healthy or making it more difficult?

Now focus on the areas of your body with pain or illness, and listen to the thoughts you are having about them.

Do you trust this part of the body?

Do you trust that it knows how to heal itself?

What thoughts are you having about this part of the body?

Do you relate to it as though it is an equal part of the whole?

Do you honor its wisdom?

What is it asking you to do?

How does it want you to relate to it and think about it?

Listen to how the body wants you to relate to it and start speaking to it in this way. What would you say to the body that would help it to heal? Any time that you think about the body or this ailing part of it throughout the day, repeat this new statement to yourself.

As we are listening to the body and what it's telling us about the state of our mind, we may hear how we think about ourselves, others, and the world and what effect those thoughts have on our body. Our illness and pain may be telling us about our wrong perceptions of reality and how they are creating harmful behaviors within us.

I had a client who couldn't sleep. He was going to doctors who prescribed him a c pap machine and sleeping pills. He still couldn't sleep. His problem was a physical manifestation of his mental world. His job was very demanding—he was in charge of many operations and people. When he woke up in the middle of the night, his mind raced at a hundred miles a minute reviewing everything he had to do and all the people he was responsible for. He once told me that he craved sleep so that he could go numb for 10 hours and experience some peace.

He was expecting sleep to bring him the peace that he needed, but in order to sleep, he first needed to find peace. If our lives never leave room for calm and quiet, when we try to fall asleep, our thoughts and worries will continue playing and keep us awake. His body was responding to his overactive mind by not allowing him to sleep. It was telling him that he needed to take care of his mental space and create more peace in his life so that his mind could finally relax.

We began our work by calming his mind and creating some mental space. We then began changing the way he thought about his work and his life. We took out some of the urgency he felt. He began to let go of being responsible for everyone else's well-being. Above all, we came back to what was most important to him: his peace. Every time he had a thought that he perceived as important, he would ask, "What is this doing to my peace and is it worth it?" He found that he had been prioritizing everything over his peace. As his intentions to prioritize peace became stronger, he was able to let go of the thoughts and worries that kept him from it. Slowly but surely, he began sleeping through the night. This shift also came with some big shifts in his lifestyle. He gave many of his work responsibilities to others and made more room in his life for self-care. His body's inability to sleep had been the final straw that motivated him to make necessary change in his life.

In order to listen to the mind-body connection, we must first observe our thoughts. In Chapter Two we talked about settling the mind and listening to our thoughts. The mind has to be settled for us to hear it. From that open space created by separating ourselves from our thoughts, we listen to our mind-body connection. As a thought comes into your mind, notice its effect on the body. Does the body tighten? Does the jaw clench? Do our hands turn into fists? Little signs from the body tell us the nature of that thought. Negative reactions in the body mean that that thought is harmful to us. If we watch on a small scale and notice that every time we have that thought we feel a surge of adrenaline through our body, this may be an indication that our inability to sleep is linked to this mind-state. If every time we have a certain thought we get a tingle of butterflies in our stomach, this mind-state may be contributing to our ulcers or heart burn.

Sometimes, as people begin to uncover these mind-body connections, it makes them more anxious. They start worrying that every time they have this thought, it is making their physical condition worse. We can avoid this by remembering that the first step to recovery is becoming aware. Awareness is a good thing. Each time you catch yourself in the middle of the thought that is surging your adrenaline, instead of feeling upset, congratulate yourself, "I became a little more aware of you today! That means I'm healing!" Noticing is a good thing rather than a disappointment.

You can practice this with the following exercise.

7.2 WHAT IS THE BODY TELLING YOU ABOUT YOUR THOUGHTS

You may want to begin with a body scan to get back in touch with the sensations of the body in non-judgment. We are not here to fix or solve, just to open in curious observation.

Now you can become aware of your thoughts. Step back from your thoughts. Do not participate in their story. Simply watch them as they come and go, manifest and disappear. As you are watching your thoughts, you may notice that certain ones play on repeat, coming up more often than others. These may be thoughts of work, your to-do lists, your regrets, expectations, or judgments. Notice what these thoughts create within your body.

Do your muscles tighten? Do you lose energy? Do you feel a surge of energy that zings somewhere in the body? Do you feel a tightness in your head? What happens to your body language? To your posture? To your facial expressions? Does your body feel good when you are having this thought?

Are these thoughts serving you?

If these thoughts are bringing up negative reactions within the body, then they are not serving you. Can you let them go? Can you loosen your grasp on them?

Every time you notice one of these thoughts, turn away from the story of the thought itself and return to the sensations in your body. Ask your body what it needs to return to peace.

Breathe peace back into the body.

Once we notice what thoughts aren't serving us, we can look into why we have them. We have our thoughts because we think they are important for something—that they are serving us in some way, keeping us safe, or meeting our needs. When we notice that a thought pattern is creating distress in our body, it's an indication that we need to re-examine why it's there and how we could alter it to serve us better.

For example, my client who was having trouble sleeping had repetitive thoughts about everything he had to do at work and within his family. He was holding onto these thoughts out of fear that if he didn't, he would let something slide and disappoint people or fail at his role in life. Fear was motivating these thoughts. When we looked into what he was fearful of, we asked if having these thoughts actually served him well in avoiding the outcome he feared. What we found is that they actually made him less likely to perform well in his role in the family and at work, because they kept him from sleeping and finding peace, making it more difficult for him to show up well for everything he was doing.

We also looked into his beliefs around his role in life. He saw himself as the head of the household—responsible for everyone else's well-being and happiness. This put a lot of pressure on him to fix their problems and be strong and centered enough to be their rock. When we asked if this belief was serving him and allowing him to show up well for his family, we found that it was, in fact, not. The pressure this belief put on him was creating stress and anxiety in his life, which made it harder for him to be truly present for his family. He couldn't really listen to what they were saying without immediately needing to fix it and then feeling disappointed when he couldn't.

We may feel like we need our thoughts for many reasons. Judgmental thoughts may serve to remind us what we don't want to do, or to make us feel better about ourselves. Angry thoughts may serve to keep us safe so that we don't let our guard down and become hurt again. Stressful thoughts may serve to keep us moving forward, accomplishing, and striving so that we don't fail. But, as we are observing these thoughts and their effect on our bodies, we may find that they don't actually serve us well at all and are, in fact, doing the opposite of what we want them to.

These thoughts may motivate us to make poor choices related to our health or well-being. For example, whenever I play sports, I have the perspective that I should be one of the fastest and best participants. If I'm going to engage in sport, I am going to push harder than anyone else. These thoughts are based on a fear of not being accepted or belonging. I think that if I am one of the best athletes, then people will accept me and I will feel like I belong. When I examine how this actually affects me, I find that I often push my body too hard and harm it. I also scare other people away, because I am more focused on being the best than on connecting with them. This thought about needing to be the best actually does the opposite of what I'm assuming it will.

You can use the following exercise to examine your thoughts and how you believe they are serving you.

7.3 ARE YOUR THOUGHTS REALLY SERVING YOU?

Start by coming back to your breath. Allow the breath to calm your body and mind. Breathe a spaciousness into your mind and step back from your thoughts. Stay in that open space behind thoughts, and observe your thoughts from a distance, not getting involved or following the story.

Notice when you have one of the thoughts that creates discomfort in the body. Listen to this thought.

What is it telling you about yourself, others, or the world?

Where did you first hear this thought?

What purpose is this thought serving?

How do you believe it will improve your experience of life or offer you positive change?

What do you think it will motivate you to do?

What do you think it will protect you from?

Now observe the actual effect it has on you. Come back to the experience it creates in your body.

How does your body feel when you are thinking this thought?

What experience does it create in your mind?

Are you open, focused, and calm?

Who are you being when you are thinking this way?

Are you able to be a peaceful kind presence for others?

Are you effective in what you are doing?

Does it create positive change in your life?

Does it serve you in a positive way?

If this thought is not serving you, can you let it go?

We have all kinds of thoughts that don't actually serve us. Negative thoughts will never disappear completely, but we can manage what we do with them. We can choose if we want to believe them and follow their story or let them go. This is a simple concept, but it is not easy. When these thoughts appear, they are very convincing. They tell us that they are very important and that we have to listen in order to stay safe. However, we know from the previous exercise that this is not true. They are not here to help us. They only harm us.

As we become more aware of their true nature, it becomes

easier to turn away. We recognize the thought, look at its true nature, and ask ourselves, "Is this really true?" We then remind ourselves that our thoughts are not the ultimate reality. We can shift them so that they serve us better. We may ask ourselves, "What thought would serve me better right now? How could I perceive this situation in a way that will motivate positive change?"

It helps to come back to our intentions, reminding ourselves what's most important. In my sports example, what was most important to me was connecting with other people and feeling accepted. If I let go of the thought that I have to be the best in order to do that and simply focus on what really matters, connection, then I will take a much healthier approach to sports. Instead of trying to win, I will focus on connecting. I won't push my body to extreme levels and harm it. I will spend more time and effort connecting with people, which will increase my sense of acceptance.

We can look at this idea in relation to my client who couldn't sleep. He believed that the pressure he was putting on himself to get everything done and always be put together would help him to show up well for his family—able to help them when they needed it. What it really did was exhaust him to the point where he was grumpy and flustered all the time. When he returned to what really mattered, which was his ability to show up well for his family, he was able to re-prioritize his life and let go of some of the things that no longer served him. When faced with his busy work schedule, instead of telling himself that he had to get it all done right away and please everyone, he would tell himself that he could do what he was capable of doing while staying peaceful and calm. This allowed him to maintain his peace, which allowed him to show up for his family as a kind and grounded presence.

Thoughts that actually serve us are ones that help us show up as the best version of ourselves. They motivate us to treat our bodies with love and compassion. They help us approach life peacefully so that we don't engage in activities and habits that harm our physical well-being. We can replace our negative thought patterns with thoughts that align with our true intentions by simply turning away from unhelpful thoughts and redirecting our attention to positive ones. There is no fight with the old thoughts, no need to push them away, or judge ourselves for having them. Recognize them, notice their true nature, let go, and turn back to the thoughts that do serve us.

You can use the following exercise to practice this.

7.4 TURNING TO THOUGHTS THAT SERVE ME

Start with the previous exercise. Once you recognize that the negative thoughts don't serve you, redirect your attention to your heart space. Remember that you are nothing but love, peace, compassion, acceptance, and gratitude. Listen to the heart to find your true values. Notice that these have little to do with how you perform, what tasks you accomplish, or what status you attain. They have to do with who you are being in the world and how you are showing up for others.

Ask yourself what you really want. Love, acceptance, belonging, safety, nourishment, peace.

What thoughts would help you to attain that?

What thoughts would help you to take a healthier approach to whatever you are doing?

What thoughts would help you to treat your body with love, respect, and compassion?

What thoughts would allow you to move forward in what you're doing in peace?

Repeat these thoughts to yourself over and over. Any time one of your old thoughts comes up, acknowledge it, recognize its true nature, let it go, and turn towards this new thought that actually serves you and your body.

8

Listening to what the body knows about the spirit

I believe that our spiritual experience affects our physical body because it helps generate our worldview and our self-image. It tells us our place in this world and our purpose within it. If our spiritual health is lacking, then our physical health will also suffer. Our physical body can tell us a lot about the health of our spiritual world. We can begin by listening to what our spirituality tells us about our body and our physical experience.

Some religions see sickness as a sign that we have sinned or lost our faith. It is a punishment for our wrongdoings. If this is the case for us, we simply observe what this does to our body. How does it make you treat your body? How does it make you relate to your pain and illness? Are you able to show your body love and compassion through this experience?

Some religions tell us that if our faith is strong enough or if we connect with someone spiritual enough, then we can be healed miraculously. There is no right or wrong answer here; I merely ask each individual to recognize for themself the effect this belief has on their physical well-being. How does it change the way you approach healthcare? What does it do to your well-being if you're not being healed? Is it working for you?

Some beliefs tell us that our physical state is a reflection of our emotional and spiritual worlds and that we can heal the physical by healing them. Again, there is no right or wrong answer. Ask yourself how this affects the way you treat your body and how you honor its experience. Does it help you to modify your lifestyle in ways that serve your body better and help it to heal? Does it motivate you to show your body love and compassion?

Some religions tell us that pain and sickness are simply a part of life and that we must bring acceptance to them in order to learn from them. Notice what this does to your relationship with your own pain and illness. Does it bring you more peace? How does it affect the way you engage with healthcare and treatments? Does it motivate you to love your body and heal?

There are many ways in which spirituality interprets and approaches sickness and pain. As you observe your own, do so with an open heart and mind willing to change if you find perspectives that no longer serve you, but also free of judgment or regret for your old ways. Some beliefs that served us well previously don't serve us any more, and sometimes we may return to old ways of seeing things that serve us better now. The willingness to change is what gives us the freedom necessary to heal ourselves in each unique stage of our lives.

8.1 OBSERVING OUR SPIRITUAL BELIEFS AROUND ILLNESSES

Begin with a breathing exercise to relax the body, calm the mind, and open the heart. Follow the breath inward and focus on the parts of your body that are experiencing illness or pain. Listen to your spiritual beliefs around these areas of the body.

What connection do you believe this physical experience has with your spiritual world?

What do your spiritual beliefs tell you this illness indicates about you and your personal spiritual journey?

Do your spiritual beliefs tell you what may be the cause of your illness?

What role do you believe spirituality plays in your healing?

What do your spiritual beliefs tell you that you need to do in order to heal?

Whose fault do they tell you it is that you are sick?

Now observe how these beliefs affect your experience with this illness or pain.

Do they bring you peace around the experience?

Do they motivate you to take care of your body and honor its needs?

Do they motivate you to make lifestyle changes that serve your body better?

How do you approach healthcare options and treatments when believing this?

Are you healing?

Observe if these beliefs are making your healing experience easier and more peaceful or more traumatic and difficult. If your beliefs no longer serve you, can you let them go?

It can be very difficult to shift our religious beliefs because we are afraid of the repercussions. Depending on the beliefs, we may feel that by disobeying them we will get sicker or will suffer worse consequences later. But, if these beliefs are creating a negative or harmful relationship between us and our body now, then they are not serving us or our future self.

I grew up Christian. The religion never fully resonated with me, but I picked up a few of the beliefs along the way. I don't think this belief is universal to all of Christianity, but I felt like God was punishing me with my illnesses. I felt like I had done something wrong and that my consequence was getting sick. This then turned into the belief that being ill was a poor reflection on me and my character. I was ashamed of being sick. I felt I carried the burden of fixing it as soon as possible so that I was no longer seen as flawed. The pressure to heal quickly and the shame around not being able to heal immediately tormented me and made healing more difficult, because I was unkind to my body and tried to push it past its limits sooner than it was able.

The next time I experienced illness, I recognized that this belief did not serve me and I began to explore new options. I spent a lot of time learning Buddhist philosophy and meditation and found a perspective that brought peace to my healing journey. I liked the idea that sickness and injury are a normal experience of life and are never a sign of an individual's unworthiness or shortcomings. I liked that it taught me to bring acceptance to the experience so that I could find peace through it and learn from it. I put less pressure on myself to heal quickly or return to "normal" right away. I gave myself permission to live the experience without hiding or denying it because of shame. For me, it was a healthier belief around illness and injury.

I do not lock myself into any one of these beliefs and know that each time I experience illness or injury my beliefs may shift again. This gives me the freedom to engage with beliefs that serve my body best and help me to heal peacefully.

As you explore your own spiritual beliefs around illness or injury, remember that what matters most is who you are being in the world and how you are treating yourself, others, and the planet. What does the body value most? When does the body feel at its best? This doesn't mean at its prime. That's different. This means when it feels most loved, accepted, and at peace, no matter what it's going through. We can be young, beautiful, and fit and still have beliefs that wreak havoc on our bodies.

We may believe that beauty is a sign of holiness and then judge ourselves anytime our body has a blemish or wrinkle. We may believe that strength and agility are a sign of power and success and condemn ourselves anytime we don't perform. A healthy value system in our physical form would be gratitude for what the body can do and recognition of all the ways the body serves us and allows us to offer our true gifts to the world, which have nothing to do with how beautiful we are or how fast we can run, but everything to do with the kind of presence we embody for others. We can be dying of cancer and still offer kindness and love to the people in our lives, and when we do, the body is at peace.

If your beliefs are motivating you to treat yourself poorly and, in turn making you cruel to others, it may be time to let them go. You can ask yourself what beliefs would serve you better and how you want to relate to your injury and illness so that you can walk through your healing journey peacefully.

8.2 FINDING BELIEFS THAT SERVE YOUR HEALING

You can begin with the previous exercise. Once you discover the beliefs that no longer serve you ask yourself, "Can I let them go?"

Remember what matters most to you by reconnecting with your

heart space. You are nothing but love, peace, compassion, acceptance, and gratitude. If your beliefs are not bringing you closer to the heart's values through your illness or injury, then they are not serving you well.

Notice if you have resistance to letting these beliefs go.

What are you afraid of? What do you think will happen if you let them go?

Is this true?

Is it worth losing your peace and well-being now?

Return to the heart again, to what's most important to you.

What do you want to be feeling through this sickness or injury?

How do you want to relate to it?

What would help you to show up as your true self even through these hard times?

What beliefs would help you to show more love and compassion to your body?

You may not know what beliefs would serve you better right now, but you can open yourself to investigating. Think of the places where you feel calmest. Think of the people who make you feel safest and most accepted. Think of the things you read or hear that resonate with your heart's values. In these places, you can begin to explore new beliefs that may serve your healing journey better.

Our physical experience can also tell us a lot about the spiritual beliefs that aren't directly related to our health, but affect it. Our beliefs affect the way we see the world and our place in it and, if this perspective is unhealthy, then our body will suffer. This is because they change the way we treat ourselves and others. They change what we say and do, and they change what stresses and burdens we carry within us. All of these things affect our physical well-being.

I had a client who often experienced migraine headaches. He was taking prescription drugs to help with the pain, but his migraines would still debilitate him for days. The experience in his body helped him to question the way he was relating to the world. He had been a Christian his entire life and worked at a Christian based school. The school along with his church believed strongly in not teaching about or supporting LGBTQ lifestyles. Yet, at home, he was adjusting to a son who was telling the truth for the first time about being homosexual. The pressure of hiding his reality at home from his nonsupporting colleagues and friends was creating a lot of stress within him. He himself was questioning his own beliefs which were telling him his son was a sinner and needed to be fixed in order to be accepted. This seemed so counter-intuitive to his fatherly instincts and what he knew to be true about his son, that he was a good person.

We began by distinguishing outside voices from his own heart's wisdom. We reconnected with his true essence, his deepest values, and who he wanted to be for his family, his friends, and his community. He remembered what was most important to him about his faith and how it supported him in his life. The most important aspects of Christianity for him were its teachings on love, kindness, acceptance, and honesty. He liked being a part of a community and feeling like he belonged. He wanted to be a kind and loving support to others and he wanted to experience more peace in his life.

We then looked at what voices did not align with his true essence and where they were coming from. He heard a lot of voices that said if he did not follow all the rules he would be judged, condemned, and outcast. He heard voices that said he was a bad father for allowing his son to stray from the Christian values. He heard voices that said love was only for those who think and live in ways that we believe to be correct, and he heard that he would lose his community if he began to think differently. You can imagine the kind of internal pressure one would feel if their life no longer aligned with these beliefs and they had to hide the truth out of fear of rejection.

We asked what these voices and beliefs were doing to his well-being. What did it feel like in his body when he was believing that he was a bad father? What did it feel like when he believed he would lose his community? What did it feel like when he believed his son would no longer be loved? We found that it brought up a lot of fear and resistance. He felt like he constantly had his guard up fighting to protect his life from the harmful effects of telling his truth. This created a lot of pressure within him and he could feel it accumulating in his head.

We then asked if this was true. Was it really true that a person was unlovable and unacceptable if they were a homosexual? Where was that true? Was that true for everyone? Was it true that he was a bad father for allowing his son to stray from the Christian values? Where was that true? Was that true for everyone? Was that true for him?

We then asked if these beliefs were helping him to be the person he wanted to be. Did they help him to live his values of love, kindness, acceptance, and honesty? Did they help him to show up as a loving and kind support to others and to experience peace in his life? The answer was "no" they did not. So it was time to shift.

We asked, "what beliefs would support you better?" He said that it would help him to believe that love and kindness were the most important thing and that acceptance was the best way to support someone. We established that love is for everyone even if they are different and that there is a place for everyone in this world. Belonging is not just for those who think like you. It's for anyone who is living as their authentic self honoring their true values. We asked who these beliefs allowed him to be, and he lit up when he said, "a really loving father to my son."

It took a long time for us to arrive here. There were many fears and doubts around shifting his beliefs. It was difficult to distinguish his own internal wisdom from all the external voices, and he often questioned which voices were his. But, once he was able to accept his son and live true to his values, the battle within him subsided. He did change jobs to work at a different school, but he still considers himself a Christian, just a more accepting one. And he surrounds himself with friends who support his true self and his son. The pressure headaches slowly improved as his life became more peaceful. This process strengthened his relationship with his son and allowed him to be the loving kind support he wanted to be.

Listening to what the body is telling us about our spiritual beliefs means asking the hard questions. What is it about your beliefs that no longer serve you? Do your beliefs still align with what you value most and who you want to be in the world. Thich Nhat Hanh has a beautiful book that he coauthored with Daniel Berrigan, *The Raft Is Not the Shore*. In this book, the Christian and the Buddhist talk about the downfalls of religion. They talk about how the shore is where our true values lie, our big "why," and the raft is the means of getting there. Religion is the raft. If we cling too tightly to the raft, then we may never step off when we reach the shore, and we may find ourselves following the raft down a treacherous river. [5]

This is what my client was facing. He was listening to all the voices that were fighting to remain on the raft and it was causing him to lose his peace and kindness. When this happens we need to step back from the raft for a moment and remember why we're on it. What were we trying to attain by participating in this belief system or this religion? What is it that we truly value most? These are always states of being, energies that we are growing out in the world. They are things like peace, love, compassion, acceptance, and gratitude. If our beliefs are making us more divisive, angry, or judgmental and are not actually generating the energies we want, then it is time to shift our beliefs. This might mean stepping away from the religion for a while to reassess, or it might mean simply shifting the way we engage with the religion. Ideally, we want to follow the beliefs that bring us more peace and turn us into the person we want to be in the world.

We can start by noticing what beliefs trigger our physical discomfort. When you think about a belief or what it is asking you to do, watch the effect it has on your body. Watch how the body responds. If the body tightens or loses energy, then you know this belief is not serving you well. The beliefs that don't align with our true values will probably cause stress, fatigue, pain, or illness in the body. These are beliefs that tell us to put up our defenses and fight, beliefs that motivate us to separate from others and condemn, or beliefs that tell us we have to put ourselves above everyone else, striving to be superior all the time. This puts stress on the body because we always have to be on edge, ready to perform, fight, and run.

We may also get in touch with the area of our body that is experiencing pain or illness and ask it what beliefs are causing its distress. When we think of certain beliefs, this area of the body may flare up or ache. These are the beliefs we need to reexamine.

You can use the following exercise to examine how your beliefs affect your body.

8.3 LISTENING TO THE BODY'S REACTION TO OUR BELIEFS

You can begin with a breathing exercise, bringing your awareness back into the body in non-judgmental observation. Get in touch with the place within the body that is hurting or unwell. You can place a hand here if you would like. You can place the other hand on your heart and feel the energies of the heart, nothing but love, understanding, and acceptance for anything that the body may tell you.

And then simply listen as you scan the beliefs that have been strongest for you lately.

When you are thinking of this belief, how does your body react?

Does this belief bring you peace and ease?

What does this belief motivate your body to do?

Does your body like this belief?

Does your body want to do what it is asking?

What is the link between this belief and the pain in your body?

Does this belief serve you and your body well?

If it does not serve you well, can you let it go?

When we observe a belief that no longer serves us, we don't judge it or ourselves for having it. It probably did serve us at one point in our lives. Fighting it will only bring more self-hatred and internal struggle. Instead, we want to turn back to what we value most. We switch our focus and reconnect with our heart's values and priorities. We may even ask ourselves what we were most valuing when we first acquired this belief and if we still value that most now.

As we become stronger and stronger in our true values, it becomes easier and easier to let go of the things that don't serve them. If we value kindness above all else and our beliefs are motivating us to judge and condemn others, then it becomes easy to release the beliefs so that we can be kind again. No belief is worth us becoming someone we're not proud of.

We also ask our body what it values most and what beliefs feel the best for it. What beliefs bring the body more peace and help it to relax. For example, my client with the migraines noticed that his belief that he could only accept and love those who followed certain Christian ideals was causing him a lot of stress. He always felt a pressure to hide his truths that didn't align and a pressure to judge and fix others who didn't align. He lived in fear of being rejected and hated himself for not being able to accept his son. When he asked the body what it really needed, it said "acceptance."

In order to feel this, he had to shift his beliefs and step

away from the people and environments that were confirming the harmful beliefs. He could be accepting if he was listening to his own heart's wisdom and what it valued most instead of to the voices outside of himself. This helped him to remember that what mattered most was to show love and kindness to his son no matter what. Now his body could relax. The acceptance helped his body let go of the stress it was carrying and he was able to reengage with peace and love.

The body points out the beliefs that don't serve us by showing how much stress and strain they put on it. When we come back to what we really value and what really matters, the body can find peace and relax. Listen to your body and ask it what values would support it best.

8.4 FINDING OUR TRUE VALUES

You can begin with the previous exercise. Once you have identified the belief that no longer serves you, stay in touch with the ailing part of your body and observe how it feels as you explore the following questions.

What value would bring you more peace?

What value would help you to relax?

What value would release your pain and tension?

What do you value most?

How can I honor your needs with my values?

Now reconnect with your heart space. This core of your being that's nothing but love, peace, compassion, acceptance, and gratitude. Ask your heart what it values most.

What's most important to your heart?

What do you truly want to prioritize?

Who do you want to be out in the world and what do you want to be sharing with the world?

What beliefs would help you to show up as that version of yourself?

Imagine yourself honoring these beliefs and these values. Picture who you would be and what you would be doing and saying.

How does this make your body feel?

9

Listening to the limitations of illness and pain

Pain and illness are not our enemy. They are a natural part of life, and they too teach us new lessons on our growth journey. The limitations that they cause in our lives may be teaching us something about needed lifestyle changes or unhealthy habits that we need to relinquish. Instead of begrudging the limitations that they put on us, we can observe them with curiosity and notice what they are saying. I mentioned in Chapter Two that we cannot listen to the body if we are fighting it. We must start by making peace with our pain and illness. You can return to that section if you need to before continuing on to this stage.

When we listen to illness and pain, we use the limitations

that they create in our lives to recognize changes we need to make. Pain indicates movements or activities we shouldn't do because they are harming our body. If we learn from pain and adjust the way we are moving or living, then we may be able to find relief. For example my back injury made it impossible for me to engage in sports at the level I once did. At first, I was very frustrated with this limitation. I wanted to ski hard and be among the best on the mountain, but this wasn't best for my body. The injury limited me so that I could develop a new relationship with sports and movement that served me better.

My client who traveled frequently to Africa for her job had varicose veins and hemorrhoids that limited her ability to sit on an airplane. When she was able to listen to the pain instead of trying to control or push through it, she discovered that she needed to stop moving so much and find peace in stillness. My client who couldn't sleep because of stress was unable to think straight or accomplish everything he used to in a day. This limitation pointed to the fact that he needed to do less thinking and striving and more relaxing and connecting. My client with migraines no longer had the mental space to judge and control others. The limitation helped him return to a more peaceful state of being. Sometimes the limitations caused by our pain or illness are indicate of what changes we need to make in our life to be well.

We can listen to the limitations of our pain and illness by first noticing them. What is changing about the way we can move, function, and interact with others? We notice what we are unable to do and all the ways we have to adapt to our new circumstances. As we notice, we try to maintain a non-judgmental state. This can be difficult if we are frustrated by our limitations, but we keep reminding ourselves that this is not a time to fight the limitations or change them, only to observe them.

You can use the following exercise to observe your limitations.

9.1 OBSERVING OUR LIMITATIONS

Start with a calming meditation. Return to your breath and remember that this is a place of calm and peace that you can always return to. Remember that you are OK, whatever you find belongs, and the heart can hold all things in love.

Scan the body and find the places of illness or injury. You may place a hand there if you would like. Be with their experience.

What is difficult for them?

What movements or activities hurt them most?

How do they affect your energy levels?

How does this affect what you are able to do?

What can't you do anymore?

What can't you consume anymore?

How does this change the way you show up in life?

Now return to the breath. Remember that you are OK even with these limitations. Know that you can find happiness even with these limitations. Relax into the present moment and turn your attention to what is good and light in your life.

We must allow ourselves to grieve the loss brought on by our pain and illness. As we observe the ways our illness or injury has affected our lives, we give ourselves the grace necessary to feel the impact. It is OK to admit that it is hard to be limited. Recently, I attended the Mountain Film Festival and watched a beautiful short film of a woman skiing through waist-deep powder in a field of aspen. While everyone else giggled with excitement, tears ran down my face. No matter how much acceptance I bring to my new lifestyle, I still feel grief for the loss of my favorite sports. I understand that skiing at that level is not best for my body and I have found new ways to bring that level of joy into my life, but that does not mean that I don't feel loss.

A balance exists between allowing ourselves to feel grief without getting stuck in it. Expressing the loss can help us move through it towards healing. If we can't acknowledge what we have lost, then we cannot find new methods to replace it. We will remain stuck in the depression and dissatisfaction. Though we lose things in illness and injury, that's not the end of the story. Transformation can come from our suffering, and we can rebuild new ways to engage fully with life.

When we feel our grief, we admit to ourselves that we are

losing something of great value. We look at the limitations in our lives and we acknowledge what they are taking from us. Then we dive deep into the emotions involved in that loss and we give ourselves permission to feel. This process can be shared with others, if they can hold a non-judgmental space of not trying to fix anything or make it better; but I find it best to be alone in these moments. I often go into nature, where I know my anger, sadness, and frustration can be held. And then I release it. I tell myself, "Be angry. Be as sad as you need to. Be frustrated. Wail if you have to. This is hard and that's OK. You have lost a lot and yes that hurts. This is causing many disruptions in your life and it's frustrating. Admit it!"

The exercises from Chapter Four help us sit with these emotions and move through them. They are here to teach us something, and to show us what we truly value and what we need to move away from or towards. I tend to scoot around my loss, downplaying the effect it has on my life, and this leaves me in denial of the holes it creates and how I need to proactively fill them. By allowing my emotions to tell me just how much I'm losing and what feels empty now, I can seek out new activities or passions that can make my life whole again.

Emotions are a good thing. They show us what's most important to us and what we value. They tell us when we need to make changes in our lives and what we need to focus on. Because of this, it is important to allow ourselves to feel the emotional side of our limitations. The emotions can help us become unstuck. They move us from the darkness of loss to the light of new growth and transformation.

You can use the following exercise to feel the emotions around your limitations.

9.2 FEELING THE EMOTIONS AROUND OUR LIMITATIONS

You can begin with the previous exercise to identify your limitations. Hold these limitations in your awareness. You can even pick one moment when you had to say "no" to something or couldn't complete something because of your pain or illness. Place yourself in that moment and, instead of denying, distracting yourself, or suppressing, give yourself permission to feel.

Place a hand on your heart and remember this safe space within you where you can hold all experiences and all emotions. Breathe into this heart space and tell yourself, "This too belongs." Allow your emotions to be present.

What are you feeling right now?

What does this limitation bring up for you?

How does it feel in your heart?

How does this emotion feel in your body?

What does loss feel like?

What aspect of this loss hurts the most?

What are you really losing?

What does that tell you about what's most important to you?

What hole is this leaving in your life?

Where do you feel empty?

What do you need that you believe you can't get anymore?

What basic need feels threatened? Love, belonging, safety, acceptance, nourishment?

Now return to the heart. Feel the heart's warmth and strength. Remember that it can heal all things. Remember that you have other ways of getting these needs met. You have other ways of connecting with joy. You have other ways of making your life whole and meaningful. Open yourself up to receiving the new, to transforming and filling your life in new ways.

After feeling the effects of our limitation it can be helpful to look into why it is so frustrating for us to have them. This is linked to Chapters Seven and Eight on the thoughts or beliefs we have about these limitations. Like we covered, the most troubling part of illness or injury is the limitations it puts on our lives. It stops us from doing our favorite activities, our jobs, playing with our kids, eating what we love, and many other things we once enjoyed doing.

For me, the pain of my back was terrible, but it was not nearly as intolerable as losing the ability to engage in the sports that I loved. When I examined why I was so frustrated to be injured, I found that being limited ate away at my joy. I couldn't do the things that made me feel good about myself, that made me feel strong, that gave me my identity, that connected me to others and to my region, that cleared my mind, and that helped me to forget my emotional baggage. I became angry at my friends when they continued doing the things that I loved and left me behind. I felt abandoned, forgotten, and useless. The limitations stole the image of who I thought I was, a strong, capable, and accomplished athlete and I didn't know who I was without that identity.

I had a client with severe back pain while raising young children. The pain prevented her from picking up her children, sitting on the floor with them, playing games with them, or doing many of the household tasks required to make a comfortable home for them. When she looked at her frustration around her physical limitations, she found it stemmed from her seeming inability to be a good mom. She looked neglectful and non-participatory in their lives. She thought she was missing out on the fun parts of being a mom and compromising her connection with her children. Her injury was taking away her ability to be the kind of mom she thought she needed to be and it was crushing her spirit.

When we start to look at the real reason we are frustrated by our limitations, we see that it has less to do with a loss of particular actions, and more to do with a loss of self-image. We are frustrated because our role in life must shift, and we can't be the same person we were before. We are frustrated because we can't live up to standards we previously put on ourselves. We are frustrated because we can't accomplish as much as we once could. We are frustrated because we have lost our source of joy. And that hurts!

Being able to see what is actually frustrating about our limitations gives us the opportunity to grow beyond them. If we stay focused on the actions we can't do, we may stay frustrated for the rest of our lives, especially if we never regain our previous physical health. If we focus on the image of ourselves that the limitations threaten or alter, then there *is* something we can do to heal. I might never be able to ski black runs on telemark skis again, but that doesn't mean I will never be strong, capable, and accomplished or that I will never feel joy. My client may never be able to lift her children, but that doesn't mean she won't be a fantastic mother. If we address the real cause of our frustration we can find new ways to ease it and continue to show up for life as our best selves.

You can use the following exercise to explore what is actually frustrating you about your limitations.

9.3 THE TRUE FRUSTRATION OF LIMITATIONS

You can begin with the previous exercise, getting in touch with what your limitations are around this illness or injury. Hold these limitations in your awareness and place yourself in a moment when you are experiencing one of them, when you can't do something, or have to give up, or don't have the energy. Feel the emotion in that moment.

Why are you really frustrated that you can't do this?

What are you telling yourself about your worth and your value?

What do you believe other people will think of you?

What expectations have you placed on yourself that you aren't able to live up to?

What do you think that says about you?

How do you believe you are failing to show up for yourself, others, or the world?

Who did you want to be that you believe this is getting in the way of?

What image of self are you losing?

Do these limitations actually prevent you from being the person you want to be?

Come back to your breath. Remind yourself that you are more than just your physical body. That healing can come in many forms. That your worth is not solely tied to what your body is capable of doing. Tell yourself that you are loved just as you are in this moment, even with these limitations.

Once we recognize why we were actually frustrated by our limitations, we can start learning from them. It can be eye-opening to see that there is more than one way to be strong, capable, and accomplished, or to feel joy, or to be a fantastic mother and that maybe these ways don't involve our bodies being perfect and unlimited. Often times the limitations imposed on us actually show us what we've been doing incorrectly and help us to remedy it. My approach to outdoor sports was aggressive, fast, and competitive. I thought that the speed and the adrenaline was what brought me joy and satisfaction. My injury forced me to stop and gave me the opportunity to reexamine how I was engaging with nature.

In the first year of my injury, I lived with a dear friend who gave me much support through my healing journey. One day I was crying on the couch because my friends were out skiing and I was sitting there in pain. She asked me if I wanted to do something, and I said, "What's the point? I can't do anything fun." She forced me to get up off that couch and hobble to the car. I was crying as we drove towards the mountains from the pain stabbing through my back. We pulled over at a snow-covered farm road just shy of the mountains. The road wove in and out of pine trees at the base of the snow-packed Collegiate Peaks. And we walked, slowly, carefully, quietly.

I cried through the first twenty minutes and then I opened

my eyes and looked around. The sunlight glistened on the snow that danced in the light breeze kissing the tops of the rolling hills. The pine bows bent under the weight of the snow creating a canopy above us. Suddenly, I found myself present for the beauty of nature, grateful just to be in its company. I began recognizing the many ways to be in nature, that not all of them involve flying down mountains at high speeds. And I felt joy. The joy of being in nature's presence and recognizing her beauty.

This started my transformation. For the next three years, I spent time in nature in calm and peaceful ways. Sometimes, I would just sit by Lake Geneva, feeling the sun on my face and watching the small waves fade into the distance and melt into the mountains. My walks were slow and allowed me to observe my surroundings. I felt more at home in nature than I ever had before. Previously, I used nature to get a thrill. I rode through her valleys and skied her peaks, but I never stopped to say thank you. I thought my joy came from the sport, but I found an even greater joy in my newfound relationship to Mother Earth.

If I hadn't gotten injured, I never would have slowed down enough to redefine my relationship with nature. If I had simply gritted my teeth and endured my recovery until I could return to "normal", I never would have discovered an even deeper joy than the one I had lost. I had to go deep into the feelings of my loss to recognize what I was actually grieving and find new ways to connect with it. It wasn't only the sports that I was sad about losing, it was the joy they brought me and the opportunity to get outside. Now I have an even greater sense of joy that comes from a more intentional connection to nature.

When my client looked into her sadness around not being

able to lift her children, she found that she was really grieving the ability to be a good mom. When asked to define what it meant to be a good mom, she said nothing that involved lifting them, carrying all of their things, or cleaning their house. It had to do with who she was being in their presence and who she was encouraging them to be. She found that not focusing on the physical movements allowed her to focus even more on the emotional and mental connections. She put all of her energy into being genuinely present for them and demonstrating what it meant to live intentionally. Being a good mom had very little to do with what her body was capable of and everything to do with how present she could be for her children's experiences and learning. This realization allowed her to engage in motherhood with confidence and joy.

Sometimes being limited helps us recognize what's most important in our lives. It can motivate us to make changes that improve our well-being and the health of our relationships. We are forced to slow down and reexamine how we have been approaching life. Often, what they force us to do is what we were actually needing: slow down, focus more on connection, prioritize mental well-being, value who we are being over what we are capable of doing, find joy in the small things, be grateful for what we are able to do, grow our spiritual strength instead of just our physical one. If we are courageous enough, we can lean into the limitations and learn how to live better because of them.

You can use the following exercise to lean into your limitations and see what you can learn.

9.4 LEARNING FROM LIMITATION

You can begin with Exercise 9.2, getting in touch with what your limitations are. Then reconnect with your heart space. Remember what it is that's most important to you, what really matters, and listen.

What is this limitation forcing you to do?

What might that be telling you about your lifestyle or your habits?

How were you approaching life before this illness or injury?

Was it a healthy way to approach life?

Was it allowing you to prioritize what is really most important to you?

Now listen again to why these limitations are so hard for you and what's frustrating about them.

What do you think they are preventing you from experiencing or being?

Are there other ways to experience that?

Are there other ways to be that?

Are there healthier ways to approach it?

Can you still prioritize what's really most important to you?

Imagine yourself being what you want to be or experiencing what you want to experience in a new way. Imagine yourself prioritizing what really matters, and recognize that your physical state can't take that away from you. Imagine yourself approaching life in a way that is healthy and balanced and that helps your body to stay well. Believe that you can still experience what you want while living in a way that helps your body to heal and stay healthy.

10

Consuming in ways that support the body

When we are healing, we have to fill our bodies with light, love, and nutrients to give them all the support we can. If we consume in ways that deteriorate our health and make more work for our bodies to cleanse, then we are counteracting all of the effort our bodies are making to heal. **During times of illness, we have to reexamine what it means to consume in healthy ways. Things we may have tolerated before may do more damage now. What used to be healthy may not be in this moment.**

When we think about what we are consuming, we are not just considering food and drink. We are also considering media, conversations, environments, and materials. It is anything that we surround ourselves with or take in through our sensory organs. Everything has an effect on our internal state and changes how we relate to ourselves and the world around us. We want to surround ourselves with things that support our healthy lifestyle and keep us motivated to be our best selves. This is crucial in times of healing because we are already struggling against many obstacles formed by our illness or injury; we don't need to make it harder on ourselves by consuming toxins from the world around us.

This process always starts by remembering what we feel like when we are at our best. This is what we did in section 6.2, getting in touch with how the body feels when it is well. We also remember what it feels like when we are aligned with our heart, which is the work we did in Chapter Five, and what it feels like to be aligned in the mind from Chapter Four. When we are aligned with the heart, there is a peace in our body and mind because we know we are living as our true selves. We understand that we are exactly where we need to be, doing exactly what we are meant to do. Remembering what this feels like helps us to distinguish the things we consume that make it harder for us to remain our best selves and those that support us.

You can begin by engaging with the feeling of being your best self.

10.1 BEING OUR BEST SELF

You can begin with a breathing and settling exercise. Bring your awareness back to your heart space and breathe into this core essence of who you are. Remember what it is that you value most, what's most important to you, and what you truly want to prioritize in life. Remember who you want to be out in the world and how you want to show up for yourself, others, and the world.

Now imagine a time when you were fully aligned with your heart's values. When you were living as your best self. If you haven't experienced it yet, just imagine what it would be like.

What would you be feeling in your body?

How would your energy levels be?

What would your body language and your facial expressions say?

How would you feel in your mind?

What thoughts would you be having about self, others, or the world?

What perception would you have of life?

How would you be relating to each situation?

What emotions would you be feeling?

How would you sit with difficult emotions?

What emotions would you be feeding?

Who would you be if you were at your best?

How would you show up for yourself, others, and the world?

Really engage with this version of yourself. Remember that it's possible to feel like this at any moment in your life if you prioritize the right things. Remember that this is who you really are.

Illness and injury change how everything affects us. Even if we think we understand how to consume in ways that support our best self, it can all change when we become sick. We consistently have to reexamine how our consumption is affecting us and how we can alter it to optimize our health and well-being. We can start by examining what kinds of food and drink we are consuming. There are certain diets that support different illnesses or injuries and can be prescribed by a nutritionist or dietitian. We can also use tests to discover low or high levels of particular body indicators. We can all build awareness of what foods serve us and which do not.

It is a matter of paying attention to what your body is asking for and how it is reacting to certain foods. When we are younger and more active, we can consume more of certain foods that we can't as we age. When we are healthy, our body is better able to cleanse from toxins that would overwhelm us when we are ill. When I was in high school, I was training for mountain bike races and playing on the volleyball team, and I had to bring a grocery bag of food to school everyday just to stay upright. Now, if I ate like that, my stomach would hurt constantly and I would gain weight. We adapt our consumption based on the needs of our bodies.

When we are sick or injured, it becomes even easier to detect which foods help us and which harm us. We may experience flare-ups of pain after consuming too many nightshades or white starches. We may experience gut pain when we consume gluten or other allergens. We may feel the effects of alcohol much more quickly and then suffer the hangover much longer. When we feel these pains, our body is telling us to stay away from these particular foods. It's alerting us to the fact that they are not serving us well and are making it harder for us to heal. If it doesn't make you feel good, don't eat it!

In my book *Living From the Heart* I wrote about how food can nourish our body but also our heart and soul, how some foods that don't benefit the body help us connect with our loved ones or spark joy in our hearts. This too shifts when we are sick or injured. Our body becomes more of the priority, and we may need to cut out more of the things that compromise it. Sugar and alcohol may have been okay to consume in moderation when we were well, but they may have a more detrimental effect when our liver is failing or we are getting early-onset dementia.

When I first got injured, I did a lot of research into an anti-inflammatory diet that would best support my nervous system. I was very sad to see that many of the things I loved were on the "no" list: sugar, caffeine, white breads, alcohol, processed foods. A more plant based diet, along with fish was recommended. I was living near the French Alps at the time, and their main staples are bread, wine, coffee, and meat. It was hard for me to find vegetarian options in restaurants, and most of my friends served meat at every meal. Letting go of coffee and sugar caused me much grief. Meat was easier for me to eliminate, but white bread? Yeah right! So I did the best I could. I cut out what felt possible and ate the rest in limited amounts. As my body recovered, I allowed myself more of the items on the "no" list, but I found that this diet served me well, and I decided to continue it even after being healed.

This also happened with a client of mine who had arthritis in her hands and knees. She followed a specific anti-inflammatory diet for arthritis. She could observe how effective it was by observing her pain levels. After eating a plate of french fries her hands and knees would ache worse than usual. When the arthritis would flare up, she would become strict with her diet and follow all the rules and her pain would decrease. The longer she ate this way, the better her body felt, and she ended up sticking to the diet even when she wasn't experiencing pain. This, of course, supports our body and helps it to stay healthy all the time making it even more enticing for us to stay with it.

Our illness or injury can actually motivate us to make dietary changes that will continue serving us in the long run. It is hard to change our diet unless we have a good reason to, and pain is a really good reason. We may have been told many times to eat less red meat, drink less alcohol, and smoke fewer cigarettes; yet until we are faced with the choice between these favored pleasures and our ability to walk, stand, or even live we may never change. So we can look at our illness or injury as a great catalyst for positive change. The diet that's recommended for our ailment may just be the diet we've needed all our lives. It may end up serving us and our planet better.

You can use the following exercise to look into how you could consume food and drink in ways that support your healing.

10.2 ASKING YOUR BODY WHAT FOODS WILL SUPPORT IT

You can begin with a settling meditation and bring your attention into your body. You can listen to the body as a whole or specifically to the part that is ailing you. You may want to place a hand either on the heart or the ailing body part. Listen deeply to the body as you ask the following questions.

What foods are you consuming that serve the body best? That help it to heal? That reduce pain and agitation? That give you energy?

What foods are you consuming that don't serve your body? Take more energy to cleanse than energy offered? Create inflammation in the body? Create allergic reactions in the body? Drain you of your energy?

These are questions you can ask throughout the day. When you eat a meal, observe in thirty minute intervals for three hours after what that food did to you. Then observe how your body feels the next day. Notice the changes in your pain, inflammation, energy, congestion, and strength.

Always return to your intentions to listen to and honor the needs of the body, knowing that this is what will bring you true well-being.

We can help our healing by being conscious of what we are consuming in television, written materials, and social media. When we are ill or injured, we may spend much more time at home. In these moments, we may reach for our computer, television, or cell phone and search for entertainment. This may be a good way to distract ourselves from our discomfort, but if we aren't careful, it can consume us and create more discomfort in our mental space.

Like I covered in my book, *Living From the Heart*, what we consume in the news, social media, conversations, television, and video games becomes who we are. It forms our perspective of the world and what beliefs we have about self, others, and the world. When we are ill or injured, our self-image is delicate. We are going through an identity crisis and trying to rework who we are within our new limitations. It would be wise for us to consume things that inspire us to continue being our best selves, even with the challenges we face. It would also be wise not to consume things that remind us of all the things we can't do and glorify lifestyles we can no longer lead.

Take the example I gave before about watching the Mountain Film Festival with tears running down my face. In Colorado, we glorify adventure sports and those who do them well. We idolize the people who can ski the gnarliest line and climb the most rugged peaks. We love to watch other people doing these sports to motivate ourselves to be that cool and capable. It is not a good idea for me to watch those films or video clips on social media. It only fuels a self-image that I'm not enough. It also fuels a belief that such a lifestyle is the most admirable and most valued by my peers. Instead of motivating me to pursue different passions and cultivate new skills, it leaves me deflated and angry.

Instead, I try to find new media sources that display people finding joy and success in music, art, writing, giving back to the world, and making positive change. These are things I can do. These are things that inspire me to seek new ways to grow and encounter fulfillment. They also help me believe that people value things other than just physical accomplishments.

I know this may sound cheesy and cliché but it's important to consume inspiring things in media. This makes a difference. If we are already feeling down and gloomy from our illness or injury, watching negative news stories will not help us feel better. It will not bring us peace to engage in online disputes over politics or social issues or to watch melodramatic television. Remember, healing happens when our minds and bodies are at peace and in a rest state. We need to consume information that helps put us in that state. We also should be especially cautious of depression because of our illness, and consuming negative media will only compound our sadness.

We want to ensure we consume information that stimulates our mind in positive ways. If we aren't getting our usual physical outlets, it helps to have more mental ones. It's good to challenge ourselves rather than be passive recipients of information. Try watching a documentary or a foreign film in the language you are learning. Listen to educational podcasts that teach you about healthy developments in the world. Play educational games on your phone instead of scrolling through mindless images. Watch videos that teach you new ways to cook or create art.

Ideally we want to spend more time creating than absorbing, so that we remember our true thoughts and perspectives rather than always taking on other people's. You may decide to create your own blog about your healing journey; even if no one reads it; it will be therapy for you. You may want to create digital art or music. A creative outlet is helpful during recovery because it gives us a way to filter our energy. It reminds us that we still have a lot to offer even if our bodies are limited.

I know how easy it can be to become a vegetable on the couch when you don't feel well, absorbing whatever appears on the television or media scroll in front of you, but in order to heal we have to proactively seek healing energy. The media can be a great source of learning, inspiration, and hope, if we look in the right places and engage in the right platforms. Don't let the media decide how you see the world. Decide how you want to see the world and what you want to be experiencing and cultivating in the world, and use the media to fuel your intentions.

You can use the following exercise to observe your media consumption.

10.3 OBSERVING HOW MEDIA CAN SUPPORT MY HEALING

You can start with a breathing and centering exercise. Recenter on your heart space. This center of your being that holds your true intentions and what really matters most to you. Listen to this heart space as you ask yourself:

What would you like to be feeling and experiencing that would help you to heal?

What mental state helps your body heal?

What thoughts and perspectives keep you motivated to engage in life?

What thoughts and perspectives inspire you to find new ways to grow and learn?

What thoughts and perspectives help you to see your value even through illness and injury?

What do you value most?

What are you deepest intentions?

Now examine what your media consumption has been like recently. Observe how many hours in the day you're consuming media and notice what effect it's having on you.

How many hours do you spend absorbing information versus creating?

How does what you are consuming make you feel? Is this what you want to be feeling?

What does it motivate you to do?

What perspective of yourself and your self-worth is it giving you?

Is it stimulating your growth and learning or numbing you?

Is it reflecting beliefs that you want to have and values that you want to have?

Is it helping you to stay positive about your healing?

Remember what it is you want to be experiencing and what you do want to be feeling. Remember what mental state helps you to heal.

How could you engage in media in a way that supports this mental state?

Consumption also refers to what we are absorbing from the environment we are in and the social circles we associate with. When we are sick or injured, these may need to shift and change. As I explained in my book, *Living From the Heart*, we absorb what is in our environment and it affects our well-being, from the sounds and air quality to the amount of light and trees. All of it changes our internal chemistry. When we are ill or injured, it becomes even more important to be in environments that support our healing. The ideal environment would depend on what we are going through.

Depending on our condition, we may need to move somewhere warmer or dryer. We may need to go where the air is fresher. Large facilities still remain in the French Alps where individuals with tuberculosis would go to recover because the air was much cleaner than in Paris. A friend of mine who was struggling with ALS was told to move to a warmer climate at lower elevation. I had to move away from Santiago, Chile, when I was developing pneumonia, because of the cold conditions and the heavy air pollution brought on by the winter's inversion effect. We can ask a doctor or professional what conditions would be best for us, as well as simply observe where we feel best. If you are struggling to breathe or sleep at elevation, you may want to consider moving lower. If you become depressed and lethargic with long dark winters, you may want to consider moving where there is more sun. If you often get headaches, don't sleep well, feel agitated and restless, you may want to move somewhere with less noise and light pollution.

No matter where you live, the best thing for healing is always nature. The more trees, the fresher the air. The quieter and more still, the more our nervous system can relax. The more natural light, the more nutrients and energy we receive. The more organic life, the more interconnected we feel. This is why Japan has included Nature Baths into their healthcare system. When people need mental or physical healing, they turn to the forests for support. When we don't feel well we need more nature than ever.

It can be difficult to motivate ourselves to get outside when we don't feel well, but remembering all the positive effects can help. We don't need to engage in a vigorous sport; being still in nature's presence is enough. Take a walk in the park. Sit on a bench to eat your lunch. Sit on your porch in the sun and listen to the birds. Drive up to the forest and just lay down on the ground. There are near infinite ways to connect with nature, and we don't have to be physically strong to do them.

When we are facing all of the changes brought on by illness, injury, or aging, we also need to consider the culture in which we live. Every town and community has its own culture. The people who live there tend to do similar activities, make a living in specific ways, eat a typical diet, and have similar worldviews. When we are young and healthy, the culture of a particular place might fit us well, but as we age or face illness, we may not fit into that culture anymore and it may cause us grief and frustration to be in a place where we no longer belong. Changing location may help us accept our new situation because we are no longer fighting against the community's norm.

This happened to many of my friends who lived in small mountain towns in Colorado, spending the summers mountain biking, climbing, and kayaking and the winters skiing. As they aged, their bodies began to feel the effects of past injuries. They no longer felt good doing all of those sports at their previous level of intensity. The cold stiffened their joints and worsened their pain. Many of them chose to move to warmer climates with activities that were less intense on the body. They moved to places where the culture revolved more around the arts, gardening, socializing, or education, rather than mountain sports. This helped them make peace with the changes they were facing because they no longer felt like they were missing out on dominant elements in the mountain culture. They found a place where the culture fit their new lifestyle better and were no longer frustrated by their inability to keep up.

I experienced the same necessity to change locations after my first back injury. I couldn't quite shake the depression I felt living in Buena Vista, Colorado. My injury prevented me from participating in my previous lifestyle which had fit the culture of the town. Being around all my old friends with their talk of powder skiing and the rock climbing triggered me. My depression was worsened by boredom. When I wasn't outside recreating, there wasn't much else to stimulate and excite me. There was no higher education in the town nor many cultural outlets. I knew that I had to move to reinvent my life.

I enrolled in a master's program in Geneva, Switzerland, and was given the opportunity to re-create my lifestyle to fit my new physical limitations. The master's program kept my brain active and engaged. The small city provided opportunities for swimming, dancing, park walks, patio dining, art shows, concerts, and many other activities that didn't require the same physical capacity as the mountains. I found friends who fit these new interests and built relationships that supported my new lifestyle. I didn't feel as frustrated by my limitations because there were so many other things I could do. My depression started to lift as my world opened with new possibilities.

We don't always have to move to re-create our lifestyle. There are ways to shift our environment by simply choosing to frequent new groups, activities, and establishments. After my first back injury, my lifestyle change felt so drastic that my current location felt too limiting. Moving to a new location supported me in making the needed shift in lifestyle. After my ACL surgery and my second back injury, I was able to stay in Montrose, Colorado. Even though it is a mountain town and most of my friends are sports junkies (including my boyfriend), I had kept enough balance in my life that I could easily switch over to prioritizing the less intense activities and still feel included in the community.

It's just a matter of placing ourselves in environments that support the healthy lifestyle choices we are making. If we are recovering from alcoholism, we don't want to continue frequenting places where we used to drink. The same applies to healthy lifestyle choices. If we can no longer do or consume things we used to, then it is best to not be in places where others still are, especially when we are first making the shift. We will build more tolerance as time goes on and it will sting a little less when someone is talking about a favorite activity that we can no longer do, but we don't want to purposefully put ourselves in triggering situations. Pick environments that make you feel good about who you are and what you are capable of doing. Choose cultures that make you feel like you belong and like you are enough just as you are.

You can use the following exercise to examine your current environment and if it is helping you to heal.

10.4 EXERCISES ON CHOOSING A HEALTHY ENVIRONMENT

A healthy environment for my body

You can begin with a breathing and settling meditation. Bring your awareness to your current environment. Notice all the different components about this environment: noises, air quality, pace of life, light quality, weather, access to nature, access to health care, etc. As you are observing the true nature of your surroundings, ask your body the effect they have on it.

Is the body at peace here?

Is the body able to relax and let go of stress?

Is it easy to feel joy in this environment?

Do you have access to everything you need in order to heal here?

Are you breathing quality air? Is that really important for your healing?

Are you getting enough sunlight if that's important for your healing?

How does the cold affect you and is the climate helping your body to heal?

Is your body happy here?

Notice if there are easy adjustments you can make to create a healthy environment where you are. Or ask yourself if you are willing to make a big change for the benefit of your health and healing.

An environment that supports my lifestyle shift

You can begin with a breathing and settling meditation. Bring your attention inward and become aware of all of the lifestyle changes you are facing due to your illness or injury. You can return to Exercise 9.1 if you need to. Now observe if the current environments you put yourself in are helping you to make the lifestyle shifts necessary to accommodate your new limitations and if they inspire you to still live your best life in spite of the changes you need to make.

Are the social settings you put yourself in associated with activities you can no longer do?

Do they inspire you to engage in new passions and activities that you can do and that help you in your healing?

Are the places that you spend most of your time filled with things that support your healing and your healthy lifestyle?

Do the businesses and establishments that you frequent support your healthy lifestyle?

If you are spending a lot more time at home then notice if you have set up your home in a way that makes you feel good about being there? Have you filled it with things that make you feel inspired and happy? Do you have places where you can go in your home to find peace and where you can be creative? Is your home clean and organized?

Notice if there are some easy adjustments you can make so that you are in environments that support your health and healing. If you found that you were in many environments that did not support your new healthy lifestyle or the shifts you need to make in your life, then are you ready to make big changes and what would those be?

11

Supporting our relationships during illness and pain

Illness and injury have an enormous effect on our relationships. Because they create major changes in our lives, we will be required to make adjustments within the dynamics of our relationships. As mentioned, we will be experiencing new emotions, routines, physical discomforts, and limitations that will change the way we relate to ourselves and others. This will challenge us as well as the ones we love.

Even though we don't feel at our physical best, we still have to be aware of how we are showing up for others. We don't have to fake happiness, but neither do we want to project our discomfort onto others. We cannot expect our loved ones to carry the burdens of our suffering. We can't throw our anger or disappointment onto others and expect it to lift from our own shoulders. The hurt we feel will only grow if we treat others poorly. It will create a schism between us and our loved ones leaving us more isolated and alone.

Awareness is the key to remaining a positive presence for others. The previous chapters help us recognize the challenges we are navigating, what we're feeling because of these challenges, and how it affects the way we show up for others. When we notice that we are struggling from the loss of a favorite activity, we must acknowledge that it may motivate us to make snarky comments or disengage when others are sharing joy. Awareness helps us recognize what we are doing in that moment. Instead of speaking harshly, we turn inward with compassion, noticing what we need so that we can nurture ourselves instead of harming others. We don't want to make others suffer just because we are. Cruelty and mistreatment of others is never justified no matter how bad we feel. All it does is spread the suffering making it grow for everyone.

My client, whose husband experienced chronic pain, suffered a lot from his cruelty. His pain showed up as anger and judgment of others. They lost their friends because no one wanted to be around him. She continued to have compassion for him, justifying his poor behavior as a result of his injury, but internally she was hurting, too. It took a huge toll on her well-being and happiness. She stayed with him and carried his burdens, but had to engage in significant personal work to counteract the harmful affects of his anger. Her own suffering made it more difficult for her to show up well for him. She was fatigued and had little energy to give to the relationship. In this way, his anger also hurt himself: because it diminished her ability to care for him, and limited his sources of help.

If we make others miserable because we are, we become surrounded by unhappy people and misery grows in everyone. We don't have to act out our pain in harmful ways. Even if we can't be cheerful and uplifting, we can attend to our internal state so that we aren't a source of negativity for others. This doesn't mean that we never get to express how hard the experience is for us or be honest about our pain. Rather, we find ways to express our discomfort without being cruel, cold, or demanding.

We start by simply becoming aware of who we are being. This is harder than it may seem. When we use our suffering to justify our behavior, or only focus on our discomfort and pain, it can be trying to turn inward and examine who we have become. It can help to take a few minutes each day to turn our focus away from our troubles and trying to solve them to ask ourselves, "Who am I being?" Often we don't want to ask this because we know we have become unpleasant, and it's easier to focus on our physical ailments than our personal behavior. If we stay focused on the way others cause our anger or frustration, then we don't have to take responsibility for our role in the experience. Yet, we are the only ones who have control over our own words and actions.

While observing who we have become, we exercise compassion. Yes, we are the ones generating this negative behavior, but maybe we haven't been aware or been taking care of ourselves in a way that would prevent it. If we look at our behavior in judgment, it will only generate more inner hatred and anger and make it more difficult to find peace. We will all have moments that we are less proud of while struggling with injury and illness, moments when we can't control our anger or our grief and end up hurting others. But we all have the capacity to forgive ourselves and make amends with those we have hurt. We are also able to take care of ourselves in a way that helps us show up more positively in the future. The first step is the willingness to look at who we are being.

You can use the following exercise to observe who you are being in your physical discomfort.

11.1 WHO ARE YOU BEING?

Begin with a breathing and centering exercise. Bring your awareness back into your heart space and remember your true essence. You are love, compassion, peace, acceptance, and gratitude. Remember that the heart is able to hold all things in love and that nothing you do or experience is too big for the heart to handle. Trust the heart to hold whatever you find in compassion.

Bring your attention away from what's happening to you. From the illness and the pain. From what others are doing for you or to you. For just these moments, focus only on who you are being. Leave behind the justifications and explanations. Leave behind the blame on others and look only at yourself and how you are behaving and speaking.

Have you been kind to your loved ones?

Have you been kind to the people helping you in all the medical centers and offices?

Have you been kind to the people in your community?

What has been the nature of your thoughts?

What has been the nature of your words?

What has been the nature of your actions?

What kind of presence have you been in the world?

What are you sharing with the world and what are you receiving from the world?

Are you being the person you want to be?

As you examine, you may notice that your mind wants to return to explanations for the difficulties of your life and your injury. You may notice all the ways you want to justify these behaviors. In these moments stay focused only on who you are being, on the choices you are making and the way you are showing up for the people in your life.

Who do you really want to be in the world?

Are you being the heart-centered version of yourself?

It can be easy to blame our discomfort on others and expect them to make it better. We may do this with our healthcare providers, our caretakers, and our loved ones. And when we aren't feeling well we may take out our discomfort on those we were expecting to make us feel better. But it's not their fault! We cannot blame our discomfort on anyone else. There may be certain things that our loved ones could do to assist us in more helpful ways-we'll get to that in the next sections- but they are not responsible for our well-being. They are not to blame for our pain and they are not the cause of our pain. We have to be aware of the sources of our discomfort so that, when we make asks of our loved ones, the asks are clear, direct, and feasible. If we are simply angry because we are in pain or suffering, there is nothing anyone can do to make it better.

When I had ACL surgery, my boyfriend moved in with me for the first time. This was a huge challenge to our relationship. Not only was he adapting to living in my house, he was also adapting to being my caretaker. He had to take on more responsibility the first month to compensate for my lack of mobility. Yet he still needed to take care of himself, going for runs and bike rides, playing video games, and working. Sometimes, as he left for a run and I was hungry and tired, I wanted to lash out at him for not being there when I needed him. I would stubbornly try to do things for myself that were beyond my capacity because I didn't want to wait until he was ready to help me. I would then, of course, end up spilling things on my wound dressing or falling in the shower, and wind up more upset at myself and him. These were internal battles I was facing and sometimes I became cold and distant when my inner angry voice grew too loud.

I had to put a lot of mindful effort into locating the origin of my real anger and it wasn't his fault. He wasn't the cause of my discomfort. I was upset at my limitations and my dependency on him, and I hated not having more control over when and how things got done. I was frustrated that I was stuck on the couch while he got to play and, instead of admitting that, I blamed him for not caring or prioritizing my needs. Once I was able to turn inward and examine the real causes of my anger, I realized it had little to do with his behavior and more to do with my frustration around my current state. I also felt vulnerable asking for things instead of simply doing them, and I felt like a burden. This made me resent my boyfriend more, for being the one I had to turn to for everything.

I discovered several real needs. I needed to feel acceptance and belonging in my vulnerable state. I needed to feel safety in the midst of my lack of control. Yelling at him or being too stubborn to ask for help would not meet these needs. What I really needed was to express my vulnerability and ask for reassurance. Once I could share my insecurity about my dependence on him, he was able to reassure me that he was not resentful and was more than willing to help me. We were able to design a schedule that worked for both of us and, at the times when he was not available, I reached out to other resources.

This kind of healing is only possible if we look inward and find the real cause of our discomfort. If we continue blaming everyone else and insisting that they need to change in order for us to feel better, then we never arrive at true resolution. The real cause is always an unmet or threatened need within us. These needs always boil down to our very basic needs of love, belonging, acceptance, safety, nourishment, and stability. When we are physically unwell, many of these needs can feel threatened and our means of meeting them will differ from when we were well.

As we adjust to meeting our needs in new ways, we feel extra vulnerable and may have the tendency to look towards others to meet the needs for us in ways that they didn't before. We may have a larger need for safety and so we turn to our loved ones to be with us more often or provide more resources for us or be stronger when we aren't. If we are unaware of the basic need creating all of our demands we may make too many asks of our loved ones, fatiguing them. If we are aware of our true needs, then we can find more resources to help us with them. We can also turn inward and recognize our ability to meet those needs in new ways.

When we look for these real needs, we have to search beneath the surface, asking "why." For example, we want our partner to be home more often to help us, so we ask ourselves, "Why do I need them to be home more often?" The answer to that may be because we need more assistance doing things around the house and can only go so long without help. Then we ask the question again, "Why do I need them to be the one helping me around the house?" The answer may be because they are the person we feel most comfortable with and who we trust to do these things. Then we ask again, "Why do I need the person I feel most comfortable with and trust the most to do these things for me?" The answer may be because we feel more vulnerable and unsafe because of our illness or injury. Now we have arrived at the real need: safety.

Safety can be re-established in many ways beyond just our partner's mere presence at home. If it is difficult for them to do that more often, now we have the ability to ask ourselves "How else could I build a feeling of safety?" If we haven't identified the real need, we may feel angry and hurt when our partner says they can't be there for us; their inability to show up threatens our basic need of safety. If we recognize our true need as the feeling of safety, not having them home, then if they can't, we can find other options to get that need met.

Knowing our true need empowers us by expanding options. If we only see our surface demands as our ultimate needs, then when these demands are not met, we feel disappointed and hopeless. By identifying the base-level need, we see that there are many ways of meeting the need, even if one option is not possible. This is key when we are recovering from illness or injury. We can feel trapped and reliant on others to meet our needs, but if we don't see one individual as our only option, we free ourselves from dependency.

If we know our true need, it also helps us communicate our requests. When we ask our loved ones to do something for us and focus on the action rather than the need, then they may feel guilt if they can't grant the request or resentment if they can but don't really want to. If we share that the requested action will help us feel safer, then they understand its importance to us; and they either feel better about doing it or can help us see that, although they can't do it, they still want to support us in feeling safe.

You can practice finding the true need beneath your discomfort with the following exercise.

11.2 WHAT'S MY TRUE NEED AND WHY AM I REALLY UPSET?

You can start with a breathing and settling exercise. Bring your attention inward and notice what you have been asking for lately. Notice what you have been wanting others to do for you and if you feel good in what you are asking for and receiving.

Do you feel content with how others are showing up for you through this experience of injury or illness?

Are there times when you feel like your needs aren't getting met and how does that affect the way you are relating to the people in your life?

Do you feel angry at them or disappointed in them when you're not feeling well?

Place yourself in one of those moments, when you felt let down by someone or were angry with them because you weren't feeling well and they failed to show up for you. Instead of focusing on what they did or didn't do, turn inward and observe what you were feeling.

What were you hoping that person would do for you?

What did you feel that would provide for you?

What felt vulnerable in you in that moment?

What felt threatened when they didn't show up in the way you wanted?

What basic need would that have met for you?

Are there other ways for you to get that need met?

Once you aren't so focused on your disappointment and anger, you can open your heart and mind to all the other possibilities for meeting that need. Look into your life and notice all the other options available to you. They may show up as people, organizations, or self-care practices. Once you know your true need, you notice how many options exist beyond that one person for meeting it.

There is a balance to asking for support from the ones we love and still being responsible for our own well-being. We have to own our healing even if we need assistance through the process. It is no one's fault that we aren't well, and it's no one person's responsibility to fix us. It's up to us to know what we need in order to take care of our well-being and ask for what we cannot do on our own.

We run into two main dilemmas when asking for help: not asking enough and asking too much. Not asking enough happens when we are too proud, too independent, too stubborn, or too afraid to ask for help. Pride tells us that we should be able to handle everything on our own and that asking for help shows weakness. We don't want our image or status to deteriorate because we now have to rely on others. Independence tells us that it's not safe or reliable to depend on others so we carry every-thing ourselves. Stubbornness tells us we are the only ones who know what's best and who can do things right so we have to keep the control in order to do everything our own way. Fear is at the root of all of these because deep down we are really just afraid that turning to others for support will harm us – either our image, our strength, our power, our control, or our freedom. In order to address all of these, we have to address our fears around asking for help.

If we shy away from asking for help, we need to look into why. We may encounter many layers before we get to the root cause. For example, we may think we like things done our own way. When we ask ourselves why we like things done our way, we find that it's because we feel like we're the only one who can do it right. Then we ask ourselves why and find that we feel vulnerable when someone wants to do things differently. Below that vulnerability is a belief that if we allow others to do it their way, we will lose our own voice and compromise our values. So the real fear is losing the ability to honor our values.

If we shy away from asking for help because we like indepen-dence, we can ask why we want to be independent so badly. We may find that we don't want to rely on anyone else because we don't trust them. Then we may find that we don't trust them because we believe that, when we start becoming vulnerable and relying on others, they will one day betray us or disappear and we will be left more vulnerable and alone than before.

All of these sources of fear can be healed. It's just a matter of acknowledging, once again, what true need feels threatened. Are we afraid to ask for help because our autonomy is threatened, or our safety, or belonging, or acceptance? Then we recognize that this need is not only met in one manner. It is not only met by this one person helping us; if they disappoint us, it does not mean that all of the autonomy we have ever had will be gone. It does not mean that we cannot find safety in other places. When we remind ourselves of that, then we can accept help without putting too much importance on the outcome. We will still be OK if help doesn't come in the way we hoped it would.

I had a client who was in an emotionally abusive relationship. Her partner would use his help as manipulation. He liked her to be completely dependent on him and used that dependency as a control leverage. When she was doing everything he deemed correct, he would assist her. If she did something that displeased him, he would take back everything he had given and make her life as hard as possible. Because she had come to depend on him for so much, when he pulled back, she felt like she would fall into destitution, unable to survive without him.

Once she freed herself from the relationship, she honored her independence above all else. She would never allow people to help her because she didn't want to become too dependent on them and lose all of her stability when they didn't come through. But when she became ill, she struggled to do everything on her own and needed to learn how to ask for help. We had to dig into her past to find the real reason she was afraid to ask for help. It wasn't just because she valued her independence. It was because she thought that it would make her rely too heavily on someone else and give them too much control over her well-being. It would threaten her entire stability and safety.

We worked on identifying the true source of safety and

stability, on acknowledging that it wasn't services provided, financial help, or material things that created her solid foundation. Her true safety came from knowing who she was at her core and recognizing that she was smart, capable, and strong and could use her resources to get out of any bind. She remembered that, even if one person didn't come through for her, she still had the ability to use her other resources and it wouldn't affect the strength she had at her center. She gained enough trust in herself and her own strength that she could begin asking for help from others.

Another client couldn't ask for help because of his pride. He had a hard time admitting he was struggling, and he ended up in the ER. He thought that he didn't want to ask for help because he was too strong and it would affect his image as all-capable; but in reality pride always hides shame or vulnerability. When we looked under the pride, we found a feeling of insufficiency, like he was never enough and he was always working to prove himself worthy.

He wanted to be worthy of his family by always being the strong one who could provide and fix problems. He wanted to be the star at work, proving his worth by never showing doubt or uncertainty. He wanted to be the most capable of his friends, always winning, always the strongest. But the real reason he wanted to do all of these things was because he didn't feel worthy of love or acceptance if he wasn't the best. There was a fear of rejection. He thought that if he couldn't show up as the best, then people wouldn't want him to show up at all. But this led him to exhaust himself and push his limits until he couldn't handle it anymore and his body collapsed. Then he had to learn how to ask for help.

We worked on finding the source of his real worth and acceptance. It did not come from him being able to DO everything right; it was inherent in who he IS. His worth was built into who he was. It had to do with the kind of person he was and what he cultivated within himself. It had to do with the love he had for others and how he shared it. He saw that, even if he wasn't performing at his best or if he needed help, it didn't change his worth. He would still be loved and accepted even if he couldn't carry everything on his own. This gave him the courage to ask for help. He was no longer afraid that it would compromise his acceptance and belonging.

When we look for the real reason we can't ask for help, we should seek the root fear, which is always tied to one of our basic needs. What need do we think asking for help will threaten? Then we remember that it's not asking for help that will threaten us. If we find our true sources of that need, we will see that no matter what the result of our ask, we will be OK.

You can use the following exercise to identify your true fear around asking for help.

11.3 FEAR AROUND ASKING FOR HELP

You can begin with a breathing and settling exercise. Bring your attention inward and examine a time that you had to ask for help. Notice how you felt about asking for help and if you were able to do it.

Why didn't you feel good about asking for help?

What were you predicting might happen if you did?

What were you afraid would happen if help didn't show up in the way you were hoping?

What did you think it would change about how you were seen?

Did you feel like it would threaten your well-being?

What basic need did you think it would threaten?

Now bring your attention to your heart space. Remember what truly creates your safety, love, acceptance, belonging, and nourishment. Remember what you know to be true about yourself and who you are. Remember that you are smart, capable, and strong and even if you need help right now, that doesn't change your worth or your ability to use your resources to meet your needs. Remember that even if help doesn't arrive how you hoped, it will not threaten who you are at your core, and you will be able to find other resources to support you.

Imagine yourself asking for help while remembering who you really are and where your true worth and safety comes from. Do you feel safer?

The second main dilemma is asking for too much help or giving away our own power in our healing. We can't give the responsibility of our healing to others and assume that they will do all the work for us. Yes, at times we have to rely heavily on the medical system to take care of us, but even in those times we need to stay active in the process. We need to observe how treatments affect us, listening to what our own wisdom tells us about our healing. No one knows our body better than we. They may understand medical treatments better, but they aren't in our bodies feeling how those treatments are received. We also have to be an active participant in the treatments, doing all we can to support our body through the process.

We have been trained to hand over our healing to the medical system. We are told that the medical system knows better than us and is the expert on all bodies. This is detrimental to our health. The most accurate information on our health comes from within our own bodies and we are the ones connected to those bodies. We have to listen to our own bodies and honor what they tell us. We should never simply depend on a doctor to fix us. We have to be involved in the process.

When I contracted schistosomiasis in Ghana, it took five months to fully develop within me. By that time, no one associated my symptoms with my travels. I was in college at the time and the first doctor I visited was part of a giant Kaiser facility. I was given a number in the waiting room, and watched for that number to appear in glowing red letters above the front desk. When my number was called, I went into the doctor's office and the first question he asked me was if I was inserting foreign objects into my anus. Granted, I had blood in my stool and was a young college student, but I felt assaulted by the question. He didn't request a stool sample or follow-up tests. He sent me home with stool softeners.

Knowing my own body, I knew that something much more was going on. My symptoms worsened and I eventually left school due to the fatigue and illness. I spent two months seeing every specialist imaginable and, at one point, was told that my illness was caused by depression and I should try antidepressants. I not so kindly told that doctor that I was depressed because of my illness, not ill because of depression. I had to continue believing my own experience and my own body, fighting for my own health, because I knew there was something else at the root of my symptoms.

Finally, an infectious disease specialist ordered a colonoscopy with an immediate biopsy so the samples didn't have time to die. My lab tech happened to be doing his master's study on schistosomiasis and recognized the parasite eggs in my intestine lining. Because they didn't have the medication for the parasite in Colorado, they gave me the closest equivalent, a horse dewormer, and within a week I was on the mend.

If I had handed over my medical care completely to any one of those doctors along the way, I would have gotten sicker and sicker, with the possibility of death when my organs shut down. It was my trust in my own body and my own experience that helped me continue pursuing my own healing. Doctors have a lot of knowledge, but they are human like all of us, with limitations based on their views and perspectives. They don't have firsthand experience of what we are going through and they aren't in our bodies feeling the difference between what we know is normal and what we're experiencing in our illness or injury. We have to be present and active in our healing journey. We have to stay in tune with our bodies and what they're asking for. And we have to advocate for ourselves when our medical providers don't provide the kind of treatment we feel is best.

Another way of asking for too much help is assuming that the people in our lives should be responsible for making us feel better, meeting our every emotional and physical need. Though we need extra support when navigating the trials of illness and injury, we are still responsible for taking care of our own well-being. We must stay aware of our needs and find resources for meeting them. We cannot depend entirely on others for our happiness and comfort.

When ill or injured, we can easily forget the trials of others, assuming that they must be in a better place and, therefore, can make us feel better whenever we need it. This is not the case. Other people are not responsible for making us feel better and, if we constantly put them in that role, it will start to fatigue them and deteriorate our relationship. Of course there are times when we will need the support of a friend to make us laugh or lighten our mood, but we have to alternate roles occasionally, remembering that we too can support them. **Nobody is responsible for making us happy. We have to do that for ourselves even when we are unwell.** The previous sections of this book teach us how to look inward and find new passions and lifestyle habits that can bring us joy through recovery. It's up to us to engage with them so that we keep living and finding happiness even in illness.

Understanding that a variety of people can support us, in our lives and our pain, can help us to identify several resources for help. Instead of expecting our partner, parent, or child to play every role in our healing, we can ask several friends, spreading out the responsibilities, or we can hire someone. Caretaking fatigue is very real and we don't want our loved ones to experience that. Asking for help is positive when we do it in a way that continues to empower us. We ask for help that gets us past a stuck spot and then frees us to continue growing ourselves. This propels our transformation to the next level, instead of enabling us to remain complacent, always relying on someone else to make us better when times are hard.

I had a client with a son who faced depression and addiction. The son would often call his family saying he had hit rock bottom and was ready to end his life. He would name the problems in his life: debt, unpaid bills, lack of a job, loss of a girlfriend, a broken truck. When he was given help in the form of money, he would simply fix his immediate problems and then return to his old ways, turning cruel to my client. His story resembled the fable of giving a man a fish instead of teaching him to fish. The help he was receiving enabled him to stay where he was. He didn't need a handout; he needed motivation to change his life. The handouts simply allowed him to stay comfortable in his situation. This kind of help keeps us dependent on our helpers, rather than empowering us to start supporting ourselves.

When asking for help, be aware of how much you are asking and why. Is the help you receive going to give you a boost on your growth journey or is it going to do all the work for you so that you can stay complacent and comfortable where you are?

You can use the following exercise to examine if the help

you are asking for will empower you or keep you dependent on others.

11.4 IS HELP HELPING OR HINDERING?

Begin with a breathing and centering exercise. Turn inward and look into the help you have been receiving through your healing journey. Notice in what ways you have been relying on others and what that has done for your well-being. Look into how it is affecting your relationships.

How dependent are you on others right now?

Are you handing all of the responsibility of your well-being over to others or are you still playing an active role in your own care?

For what specific tasks or activities do you rely on others?

Why do you need someone for that task?

Is their help giving you just enough so that you can empower yourself to keep growing and learning?

If you are dependent on others for much of your physical care, are you still working on your emotional, intellectual, and mental growth and well-being?

Are you spreading the helping tasks out to a balance of friends, family, and professionals or are you depending too heavily on one?

Can you tell if your loved ones are getting caretaker fatigue?

Is the help making you more empowered and self-sufficient or more complacent and dependent?

Do you think you're asking for more help than you need?

Remember that, even if you need help in certain areas of your life, you are still strong and capable in many ways and there are always things you can do to keep yourself healthy and well. Remember that the person who has the most control over your well-being is you. Remember that your own will to heal needs to be stronger than the will of all of your helpers, and you should be putting in the most effort of anyone.

What's one thing you could do for yourself that would further you along on your healing journey and increase your well-being?

Receiving help and support from our loved ones can be just as difficult as asking for it. Graciously receiving help is a very large lesson during illness and injury. Sometimes, because we are embarrassed about our needs, we shut down when others are helping us. We don't thank them or honor what they are doing for us because we wish they didn't have to. Or we become angry and controlling about the way they help us. Accepting help does not make you weak, shameful, less valuable, or unworthy. These are the feelings that make us act negatively when receiving help. They make us feel bad about ourselves so we end up being cruel to the ones helping us. By healing these feelings and recognizing the growth potential in both giving and receiving help, we can accept the assistance we receive with an open heart.

It helps to observe how we are receiving help. Do we look down and shy away from being in the situation? Do we become angry and controlling? Do we make jokes and avoid hard moments? All of these reactions may indicate the same kind of resistances that we found in the section on asking for help. They show us that we think our worth, belonging, safety, acceptance, or autonomy are at risk because someone else has to do these things for us. When we act out of these fears, we don't treat our helpers very well.

In order to receive help graciously we have to feel confident in ourselves and in our own worth. We have to know that accepting help is a sign of strength, not weakness. We have to remember that we are using this help to better ourselves and to empower ourselves on our own healing journey. When we are confident in these truths, we can receive help without feeling threatened.

Receiving help graciously doesn't mean we have to deny that it is difficult to have someone else wipe our butt or assist us in the shower. Adjusting to this kind of humility is hard. We can admit that. By admitting that openly, we don't have to act out against our helper to prove it. Share with them. "This is hard for me. I'm not used to having people take care of me. I feel vulnerable." Just saying this out loud releases it from our own hearts so that it doesn't fester and turn us cruel. Then we remind ourselves that we are still worthy, we are empowering ourselves on our healing journey, and accepting help is a sign of strength, and we move from the humiliation and embarrassment to gratitude.

It is not easy for our helpers to do many of these things for us. It puts them in a position as awkward as ours, and both parties are adjusting to the changes in dynamics. Instead of making it harder on them by allowing our discomfort to manifest as negative behavior, we move towards gratitude. We can acknowledge what they are doing for us and thank them. We can openly discuss what makes it difficult. We can admit that we are more dependent on them right now and talk about how that affects us. But, most importantly, we stay in a mindset of gratitude.

We also want to focus on who we want to be in our relationships with these individuals and what we would like to experience in that connection. In a healthy situation we want to feel cared for, safe, loved, heard, and accepted and we want to offer those things in return. We may believe that our dependence on others' help makes them love us less or lessens us in their eyes. This can cause us to lash out or push them away when what we really want is to be close. Our fear response to feeling vulnerable actually creates the situation we feared. So we remind ourselves of what we really want to experience and recognize what approach to vulnerability will be most beneficial. This approach almost always includes honestly admitting what's hard, asking for what we need, and accepting it with gratitude.

While I was healing from ACL surgery it was hard for me to allow my partner to do all of the cooking, cleaning, shopping, and laundry, to allow him to help me into bed, bringing my ice and my pills, putting on my shower sock, and assisting me in and out of the tub. My embarrassment made me want to push him away so that I didn't have to face the humiliation of being so dependent, but that only made him less willing to help. I also tried cracking jokes which worked to keep the mood light but didn't get to the bottom of what I was feeling. What proved more beneficial was admitting how hard it was for me to accept help and explaining that that didn't mean I wasn't grateful. This helped him to understand that I was upset at the situation, not at him, and that I was really honored he cared enough to help me. He was then more willing to stay present in those tough moments, and I could direct my discontent at the situation instead of at him.

You can use the following exercise to examine how you receive help and where the difficulty lies.

11.5 RECEIVING HELP GRACIOUSLY

You can begin with a breathing and centering exercise. Turn your attention inward and observe how you have been receiving help. Notice how it makes you feel to rely on others and who you become in those situations.

Do you disconnect when receiving help and avoid eye contact or conversation?

Do you become angry, critical, and controlling of how others are helping?

Do you avoid the difficulty with humor?

What underlying insecurity or fear are those tactics hiding? These may go back to the ones you found in the section on asking for help.

How do these insecurities and fears make you behave towards your helper?

Is this helping the situation or making it more difficult?

Is this behavior getting you closer to what you want to feel?

What do you want to be experiencing or feeling?

What would help you to get there?

Now get in touch with your gratitude. Recognize all of the assistance that this person is offering you and how much that really means to you. Recognize what that assistance will allow you to do and how you want to use it. Express your gratitude to the other person.

We all know that communication is one of the key components to a healthy relationship, but communication gets more challenging when we're facing new obstacles like illness and injury. We all respond in different ways when we're going through something difficult. Some of us close off and shut down. Some of us attach more firmly. Some of us feign indifference or act like nothing is wrong. And some of us become hostile. Many of these changes have to do with the same causes discussed in the section on noticing who we become when sick or injured and are often linked to our own fears and unmet needs. What helps us to work through them with our loved ones is to communicate our internal experiences. Understanding is the foundation of love, and we can't understand one another if we aren't communicating what we're really going through.

In order to communicate what we're going through, we have to understand it ourselves. That's the purpose of the first nine sections of this book. Use them to understand why this experience of illness and injury is hard for you and identify what feels hurt or vulnerable so that you know what you need to communicate with your loved ones. We want to share our truth with the people we care about most, the ones who are present in our lives and who are walking this recovery journey with us. Sharing will help them better understand and know how to support us. That way, when we have hard moments and act out against them, their understanding of our experience and needs will help soften the hurt they feel. If we simply act out without explanation it feels a lot more bewildering and painful for the people in our lives, and they feel less equipped to handle it.

We may feel we are protecting the people we love by not sharing our inner turmoil or pain. We believe that putting on a happy face will make the situation less uncomfortable for the people around us. But this just makes it more confusing for our loved ones. They feel misled and shut out, and they grow more hurt when we act out in our hard moments, because they don't understand why. It is beneficial to everyone if we share our fears, needs, vulnerabilities, griefs, and struggles. Most of the time, others already know that we're going through a hard time. Trying to hide it only builds walls of deception.

Sharing our vulnerabilities is not acting out of our vulnerabilities. When we communicate our pain, we do so out of love and it creates connection. When we act out of our pain, it's harmful and we lose connection. Communicating pain means we are aware of what hurts, why it hurts, and what we need. When we share, it's explanatory, not reactionary. Acting out of pain means we know we're in pain but we don't understand the real cause or our needs, and we release that pain onto others in harmful ways like yelling, condemning, or blaming. We don't have to project our pain onto others in order to communicate it.

We always start healthy communication by returning to self and observing what's really going on within us. This gives us time to calm the harmful feelings and look into what's causing them. We come back to a centered state in which we can clearly communicate out of love and with the intention to connect and generate more understanding. We have no expectation that our loved one will fix our pain or that they are to blame for it. We remember that only we are in control of our happiness and well-being, and we are simply sharing our needs with others so that they understand them better. It is then up to them to use that understanding to help us. When we understand our needs, we know we can find the resources to meet those needs whether or not our loved one can help in this moment.

In loving speech, we want first to express that we are

struggling, and share our feeling, then share the threatened need that's creating that feeling, and finally end with what we need in order to feel better. For example, "This is hard for me because I am feeling ______. My need for ________ feels threatened or vulnerable and what I really need is ___________." Sometimes we may not be at the point where we know all of this. All we know is that we don't feel good. We can share that, too, followed by the intent to take care of our emotion and understand it better. Maybe we need to ask for space so that we can do that. What we want to avoid is sharing that we feel bad, followed by a demand that the other person needs to fill in order to make us feel better. Communication is not demanding or blaming; it's sharing with the intent to increase understanding.

When we share in this way we are inviting our loved ones into our experience. We're telling them that we trust them with our vulnerability and that we want to help them understand us better. We're communicating in order to increase understanding and connection between us. By sharing our feelings, their root cause, and the need behind them, we show our loved ones that we have done the work to understand ourselves. Rather than simply sharing our pain with an expectation of what they should do about it, we take ownership of the experience and healing, and ask them to be a part of it. This takes the pressure off of them and invites them to support us along the journey we're taking towards healing.

You can practice this form of communication with the following exercise.

11.6 COMMUNICATING WHAT'S HARD

Before sharing with others what you're struggling with and what hurts within you, first turn your attention inward and give yourself a moment to recenter and reconnect with your inner state. Ask yourself if you really understand what's causing the suffering within you. You can go back to the section of the book that addresses what you're struggling with and use those exercises to identify what's at the root of your discomfort. As you do so, make sure you can answer the following questions.

What is the feeling or emotion behind your suffering?

What is the vulnerability causing this emotion?

Which of your basic needs feels like it is threatened or not being met?

What do you need in order to meet that need?

You can share that with others out of love.

When we are sick or injured it can be difficult to give empathy to others. Our own suffering takes all of our attention, and we only think about what we need and why we're hurting. We get lost in our own experience and forget to think about anyone else. We may also avoid listening because we don't want to hear one more need that we don't have the energy or capability to meet. But, in order to stay connected with the people in our lives, we have to spend time listening to them and practicing empathy for them. It can't be all about us. It is very healing to recognize how our own suffering can increase our understanding of the suffering of others, growing our empathy.

Our healing journey includes the people in our lives. They also experience changes and challenges because of our situation. They may be grieving the loss of the partner, colleague, parent, or child that they knew before the injury or illness. They may feel resentment and anger at the extra duties they have to assume. They may experience fear for what these changes may mean for their future. On top of all that, they still face the usual challenges in their own lives, still experience the ups and downs of everyday life.

Like I've said before, love and connection are about understanding, which doesn't work if that understanding is one-sided. We have to listen to the other people in our lives so that we understand what they are going through during our sickness or injury. We have to be open to hearing their difficulties and their needs. This can be challenging because we can feel we have no extra room for the needs of others when our lives are in chaos. **Listening doesn't mean that we are taking on the responsibility of fixing. When they share their struggles and needs, the main goal is to help us understand what they're going through, not to meet all of their needs ourselves.**

Listening to others helps us recognize that we are not the only ones facing challenges. It opens our hearts and minds to the experience of others. This helps us to understand their behavior and how much they are able to offer. Listening also helps others feel valued and respected. It helps them feel seen even when our illness or injury seems to be taking priority.

It can be hard to listen when their struggles are related to our condition. We may interpret it as an attack against us, one more thing we're failing at while sick or injured. It is important to remove ourselves from the center of the story. Allow them to share openly and honestly, knowing that, although they may be struggling with our situation, it is not our fault. This listening time is about them and their experience. We want to listen from the heart with the intent to understand them better.

While listening, we allow lots of space and time for them to share completely before responding. We don't want to jump into explaining ourselves or why it's hard for us or why we can't change it right now. We don't want to focus on fixing the situation or solving the problem. We just want to listen so that they have time to express their feelings and needs. When they express a need, we may feel ourselves tense up because we feel inadequate in our inability to meet that need. Remember listening does not mean we are taking on the responsibility of meeting the expressed needs. Listening only increasing understanding. Expressing the need out loud will help the other person feel validated and can empower them to find the resources they need.

We may have to ease into listening gently. There may be things that are hard for us to hear. As we listen, we observe the effect of what we're hearing on our body, mind, and spirit. We notice if we start to tense up and close off. We notice if our limbic response kicks in and we feel the urge to fight, flee, or shut down.

When it is too much for us, we can ask to take a break and come back later so that we don't respond in harmful ways. Always return to what really matters while listening, understanding the other person better; then we don't feel the need to defend ourselves, change their perspective, or fix their problem. This makes it a lot easier to listen through hard moments, repeating to ourselves, "I'm just here to understand. This is not about me."

Once we have heard the other person's experience, we can practice empathy. We acknowledge that what they are going through is real and we try to relate. All we really need to say is, "That must be really hard." Everyone experiences suffering but we try to avoid comparing. There's no way to compare situations of suffering. Everyone will relate to their experience differently and may be feeling more intense emotions around it than we think. We may feel like our suffering is larger, but that doesn't make theirs any smaller. We have to allow them their experience.

Comparing kills connection. It keeps us at the center of every conversation, always bringing it back to how we see it or what we're going through when what we really need to do is give the other person permission to have their experience. Even if we aren't vocalizing our comparisons, they might be going on in our head. We are listening to our loved one explain what's hard for them while the dialogue in our own mind is, "Oh poor you, imagine how I feel. I'm the one in pain all the time or losing myself to illness." When this dialogue is playing within us, we can't hear anything the other person is saying. So we quiet the comparing and openly accept their experience.

I struggle with this a lot when my back pain is intense. My partner will be sharing about his muscle soreness from over-skiing or over-lifting, and all I want to say is, "You brought that on yourself from playing too hard." I don't want to hear about how skiing all day made him sore when I hurt all the time from sitting. This comparing undermines his experience and brings the conversation back to my own suffering. Instead, I take myself out of it. I don't use my own experience as the center point of reference. I let his experience stand alone, because in his world it is a big deal and I can allow him that experience.

It was also hard for me to hear my partner share about the burden of his extra tasks while I was recovering from ACL surgery. When he expressed that it was hard for him to cook and clean, the first thought that went through my mind was, "I used to do both all the time, and just imagine what it's like to not be able to stand for more than five minutes without shooting pains and to have to be at the mercy of everyone else to get what you need." Yikes! That internal dialogue did not help me hear or honor his experience. For him, his struggle was real. This was a change in his routine and his normal work load. It did take away his free time to relax and recuperate. It did put more weight on his shoulders. When I was able to hear that and empathize with him, it freed me from the guilt I felt around having him do these things. We could talk openly about what he needed in order to feel supported, and it made our connection stronger. Otherwise, we would have simply continued pushing one another past our limits and feeling anger and resentment.

Listening to another person's suffering through our own can be hard at first, but the understanding it builds supports a healthy connection. It allows each person to feel heard and seen and helps us to work together to improve the conditions for everyone.

You can practice listening with the following exercises.

11.7 LISTENING THROUGH SUFFERING

You can begin with a breathing and settling exercise. Reconnect with your internal state and observe how this state is changing throughout the whole exercise. Notice how you are doing in this moment and make sure you are in a centered and stable state. Don't lose contact with how you are feeling as you open to listening to another person. When you open the conversation, you can start by letting them know that you love them and want to hear their experience. Ask them how they are doing and just listen.

Notice if you start to close down or become defensive. You may feel it in your body first if it becomes tight or surges with energy. You may notice it in the thoughts you are having. If you need to take a break from listening, tell your partner you will return to listening later.

As they are sharing, notice if you are formulating a response in your head: trying to fix, solve, justify, or deny. Remember that this is our way of making the story about us. Take yourself out of the center of the story and remind yourself that this is not about you. You are here to hear their experience.

As they are sharing, notice if you are comparing their suffering to your own. Notice if that dialogue is playing in your head, undermining their experience with your own. Quiet this dialogue and remember that this listening moment is about them and allowing them to have their experience.

Once you have heard their experience, thank them for sharing and express that you have heard them by repeating what they said they were feeling and needing. Use that information and the information from your sharing in the previous exercise to work through ways to support one another as you move forward.

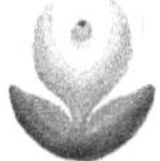

When we are stuck in pain or illness and our limitations are stealing our motivation and energy, it can feel like we have lost our value to others. We may feel useless to the people around us, which makes us close ourselves off and isolate. If we can't serve in the ways we used to, then why show up at all? But we always have value.

Our role in a relationship may shift and change when we are sick or injured. We may not be able to show up in the same way we once did, but sometimes this helps to deepen our relationship by showing us we have value outside of what we are able to "do" for the other person.

I had a client who was a doer and who linked her worth to what she was able to do for others. She would bend over backwards to meet the needs around the house: the laundry, cleaning, cooking, shopping, and on top of all of that, she was also in charge of their business. She had the impression that, if she stopped doing these things, the people in her life would stop loving her. When she had to have surgery and take a break from all of the doing, she felt panicked. How could she take a break? Everyone needed her and that's what made them love her.

We worked on redefining love. Love isn't about what we "do" for others; it's how we make them "feel." Love is based on the kind of person we are being, not on the tasks we are completing. It has to do with the way we see the other person and support them in living their highest self. It's about sharing experiences of growth together and watching each other evolve and transform. Love based on acts of service alone is not true love. Even if we can't actively do things for the people in our lives, we can still show up for them in the way we listen, share, reflect, support, and more.

After her surgery, she took two months to recover and in that time had to limit what she was doing. She had to let go of a lot of the chores she did around the house, and she was unable to go into work. The experience was quite healing for her, because she got to recognize her worth outside of what she was capable of "doing." She saw that people still loved her and still valued her, even if she wasn't serving them. Her husband picked up more of the slack, and they were able to deepen their connection because she was able to focus on ways of loving beyond serving.

We all fear that if we can't show up for people in the way we used to that they will stop loving us because we are no longer of value to them. **Healthy love has very little to do with services and tasks and everything to do with who we are at our heart's center. If we are loving, kind, and true to ourselves, then**

we will always have value in a relationship. Our value comes from the kind of presence we are for others. Can we listen to them deeply? Can we feel compassion for what they are going through? Can we hear their heart's desire and remind them of it when they have forgotten? Can we still grow together towards shared values? If so, then we still hold value in the relationship.

You can practice this now with the following exercise.

11.8 YOUR VALUE IN RELATIONSHIP

You can begin with a breathing and centering exercise. Return to your heart's center and reconnect with your true essence. Remember what you value most and what's most important to you. Remember that this has nothing to do with what you are able to "do" physically and everything to do with who you "are."

Explore what you think you are valued for in your relationship.

Why do you believe you have worth for your loved ones?

Do you think they love you because of what you do for them?

Do you think they love you because of what you can provide physically?

If this is the case, how do you feel in that relationship when you are sick or injured and can't do those things?

Return to the heart space and examine your relationship from the heart's perspective.

What worth does the heart believe you have in the relationship?

What does the heart think forms true connection?

What does the heart think you have to offer in this relationship?

Can you still spend time listening to their hopes and dreams?

Can you still listen to their suffering and hold it in compassion?

Can you still share common values and grow towards living them?

Can you still know their heart and help them to find it when they have forgotten?

When you are connecting with one another through the heart, you hold value no matter what your physical body is capable of giving. Know that you still have value in the relationship even when you are sick or injured.

There is no doubt that when our pain or illness is sucking up most of our energy we don't have a lot to give to other areas of our lives, including our relationships. We start expecting those areas to refuel us and feed us instead of us giving to them. But our relationships will suffer if we don't continue to nurture them. It is still important to engage in joy within our relation-ships, even when we aren't physically well.

Joy is one of Thich Nhat Hanh's four components of true love. He describes joy as engaging in play, laughter, discovery, and learning together. This nourishes our hearts and spirits and keeps our relationship fresh and interesting. It helps us to remember and engage with the light side of our partner. It waters all the good seeds within us and helps our happiness grow. Illness and injury can consume us. It can take all of our time and mental capacity, leaving little room for anything fun. Yet fun may be just what we need in order to heal. [6]

The depression we feel when we're unwell can actually prevent us from healing. I explained this more in my book, *Living From the Heart*. Depression suppresses our immune system and our motivation to engage in activities that nourish our bodies. By intentionally engaging in joy, we support the healing of our bodies.

Joy is the childlike wonder within us. It's the ability to see everything in life as though discovering it for the first time. Everything looks like a miracle when you've never seen it before. We let go of judgment and the adult facade of having it all figured out and we just play. Joy can come in the simplest forms. We can play a game together. We can learn a new language or a new skill. We can try new foods. We can watch comedy. We can play music. We can do anything that takes us out of the everyday routine. We don't have to go on big adventures and do difficult activities. Joy can be anywhere; we just have to actively engage with it.

I was always under the impression that joy in relationships

came from being able to do big things together, like ski trips, backpacking adventures, and travels to foreign countries. I failed to see the possibility of joy in simplicity. So when I was injured, I figured there would be no more joy in my relationship. But I discovered that joy can be present in the little things. Some of the most fun I have with my partner is when we cook a new dish together or when we try a new restaurant. I love playing games and music with my partner (even though we do get rather competitive in both). Even reading new books and then discussing new topics can bring joy.

When my partner and I are tired from the stress of the day, it can be hard to motivate ourselves to do anything but turn on the television. But, this does not feed the joy in our relationship. So we intentionally make dates to do a different activity. It keeps us interacting in new ways and learning more about one another. It helps us to see each other in a new light and keeps the relationship fresh.

Joy is not only present when everything in our lives is perfect and we are healthy and whole. It shows up when we choose to feed it. When we choose to engage with the wonders of life present for us at each and every moment, joy arrives, and shared joy creates strong bonds.

You can practice engaging with joy in your relationship with the following exercise.

11.9 ENGAGE WITH JOY

You can begin with a breathing and centering exercise. Turn your attention inward and engage with a sense of joy. If you don't have one now, then recall a time when you did feel joy. Remember what that joy felt like in your body, your mind, and your spirit.

Now ask yourself if you are feeling joy in your relationship.

Are you actively engaging in activities that cultivate joy?

Have you let your pain or illness take the joy away from your relationship?

Explore the different activities that bring you joy: discovering something new, learning, playing, laughing, exploring. Focus on the ones that you can do now. Remember that even simple things can bring you joy.

Is there one of these activities that you can do with your partner or loved one?

What do you enjoy doing together?

When can you do this together?

Set an intention to engage with joy with your partner in the next few days. Make a regular time each week when you can continue to do things that bring you joy together.

12

Our Work and Purpose During Illness

Illness and injury can easily steal our jobs and our sense of purpose. They take time and energy away from our work and can render us incapable of performing our usual duties. This brings up its own level of fear, anxiety, and depression. Many people get their sense of worth and purpose from their job. When that job is compromised, their identity unravels, and they fear losing the money and safety that a job provides. If we can't work, who will provide for us?

These fears lead many of us to continue working in positions that compromise our health. We ignore the signs of fatigue or hide our true needs so that we don't lose work. All the while, our illness or pain is increasing until we can't handle it anymore.

In order to heal, we have to be honest about what our job is doing to us and whether we can handle it in our current state of health. We want to watch for prolonged stress, exhaustion, repetitive movements that aggravate our pain or injury, toxic environments, and emotional overwhelm. If our job is a source of any of these things, then we need to consider a change in order to heal.

This is what my client faced when her body told her she could no longer work in Africa. She tried all kinds of remedies that would allow her to continue her work, but the ailments kept coming back. She had to work through the fear of losing her sense of self, her sense of purpose, and her income in order to make the necessary choice to prioritize her health. We began by recognizing the toll the job was taking on her body. She listed all of the physical demands her job put on her body: taking long flights, losing sleep for days, eating unusual foods, sleeping on the floor, using outdoor toilets, carrying heavy luggage over rough terrain, standing for hours, and more. Then she looked at the recommendations for her ailments: rest, not taking long flights, not standing in one place for too long, and not carrying anything over 30 pounds and saw that her job, as it was, would not allow her to follow those recommendations.

We then looked into what the job was doing to her mental and emotional state. The long months in taxing environments were causing her a lot of stress. She no longer felt aligned with all of the company's values which caused an internal battle within her. Having to leave every three months was creating unrest in the rhythm of her life. She was feeling stressed, exhausted, and emotionally drained. This negative mental state made it hard for her body to heal. Simply observing the reality of her job and the effects of it on her body motivated her to work towards change. She recognized the disconnect of craving the adventure the job provided, while, at the same time, suffering from the physical and emotional consequences of travel. It was time to make a shift.

The process of making change in our work starts with observing. We approach the observation with an open mind and heart. We don't have to make any big decisions right away. We don't have to judge ourselves for the situation we are in. We simply look at our work experience with curiosity wanting to truly understand how it affects our health.

You can practice this now with the following exercise.

12.1 OBSERVING THE CONDITIONS OF MY WORK

You can begin with a breathing and settling exercise. Come back into a state of non-judgmental awareness. Let go of your need to change, fix, or solve anything right now. Just observe the truth around your job and how it is affecting your well-being.

You can begin by noticing the physical activities you have to do at work.

What movements do you make all day at work?

How does your body feel while you are at work?

Do any of the movements aggravate your pain or illness?

Are you able to rest enough at work?

Are you able to move enough at work?

How is your job affecting your physical body?

Now you can look into your mental state while at work.

How are your stress levels at work?

Do you still feel work-related stress when you go home?

How is your emotional state at work?

How do you feel when you think about work?

Do you feel mental fatigue at work?

Now you can look into the state of your heart and spirit at work.

Do you align with the values of the company you work for?

Do you feel valued and seen?

Can you share your true thoughts and feelings?

Do you feel respected?

Do you feel a sense of connection at work?

How is this work affecting your illness or injury?

Is it helping you to heal?

If we want our bodies to heal in a sustainable lasting way, we have to heal every aspect of our lives and that includes our work. In order to make the necessary changes to our job, we have to remind ourselves what's most important. This can be difficult when it comes to a job because we link our job to our most basic needs, safety, and nourishment. If we don't have an income, we can't provide for our most basic needs. Often this trumps all health needs, and we stay in positions that are compromising our well-being.

I always encourage people to look at the bigger picture. If we continue down a path that compromises our health, then eventually we could be in a position in which we can't take care of ourselves at all: a mental breakdown, an incurable disease, or a chronic injury. It could potentially affect us for the rest of our lives. Making a hard choice now could save us from detrimental consequences later.

Trust can also help us in these moments. We have to trust that if we make choices that prioritize our well-being, they will lead us to new possibilities that serve us better. Thich Nhat Hanh always said that happiness is not the destination, it is the way. I think about health the same way. If we keep pushing through unhealthy conditions, thinking that one day we will arrive at health, we'll never get there. If we make health the way, then each step we take will be cultivating the health we need to live as our best selves. We can't perform in life and do all that we're meant to do if we are mentally and physically unwell. The consequences of prolonged illness or injury would probably render us incapable of working in the future anyway, so prioritizing health now is the only way to build a healthy future.

This switch in perspective took a while in my client. She kept returning to the financial security that her job provided her. Fear kept her from seeing other possibilities. She thought she was too old to find a new job, needed more to survive than retirement would provide her, and wouldn't be accepted if she asked for a lighter load. This kept her locked into a position that was compromising her health. We started by shifting her perspective on what was most important to her. Was it the income or her health? How would poor health affect her income? What quality of life would she have if she kept working this job now, but compromised her health for the future? She recognized that her health was her biggest priority. If she wasn't well, then nothing else would matter. We started making choices that would prioritize her health.

Trust was the next step. Money fears are real. They can control our every decision, because we know that if we don't have money, we can't survive in this world. We also need money in order to heal and often we need the insurance that our job provides to get necessary medical care. This is a horrible trap. We feel like we have to keep doing the thing that is making us ill so that we can afford the care to get better. When we step out of fear, other possibilities open up for us. When we choose to prioritize well-being, new paths begin to emerge. **Trust doesn't mean that we sit on our haunches and wait for everything to resolve. It is a confidence that if we continue to make choices**

that prioritize our well-being, each step will bring us closer to healing.

This trust opened her mind just enough that she could see new possibilities. She looked into alternative forms of health insurance and went over her budget to see what she needed to eliminate in order to retire early. The numbers began to align, and it suddenly felt attainable. She made the choice to quit her job and take time to heal. And heal is what she did. Within two months, she was feeling better and within two years, she was living her best life.

Whether we have to take time off, change our role, or change jobs, knowing what we truly prioritize and trust are the first building blocks for that change. Knowing our priorities gives us confidence in the choices that we are making, and trust reassures us that those choices will lead us where we need to be. If we prioritize our health and well-being, then each choice we make will help them grow making it easier for us to live as our truest self.

You can use the following exercise to set your priorities and trust.

12.2 BUILDING CHANGE ON OUR PRIORITIES AND TRUST

You can begin with a breathing and settling exercise. Place your attention on your heart space. Feel this center of your being where your true values reside. Know that this is your true essence and what really matters. Ask your heart what matters most to you.

What do you truly prioritize?

Who do you want to be out in the world?

What do you want to cultivate within you so that you can share it with the world?

What allows you to be your best self?

Now look into what you have been prioritizing in your work and your life.

Have you been prioritizing the values of the heart?

Have you been led by the heart or by fear?

Has each choice you've made aligned with your true values?

Are you making choices that don't align with the hope that you will eventually arrive at what you truly want?

What effect is this having on your well-being?

Is this helping you to be healthier now?

Return to your true priorities and remember what you want to grow in your life. If you want health and well-being then every step you take has to prioritize that. If you are making choices that prioritize your true values, that is what will grow. Trust that, by taking care of your health, you are taking care of your future. Trust that, when you are taking care of your health, you are taking care of those around you. Trust that, when you have well-being, you can show up as your truest self.

Now that we understand our priorities, we can be honest about what we need at work. This is hard for me. Admitting my limits feels like admitting defeat. It feels like giving into my illness and allowing it to control my life. I tend to push through my pain and fatigue to prove that I can. This never ends well for me. I never fully heal. It actually takes more courage and shows more strength if we are able to ask for what we need and honor our healing process. Healing then happens more quickly, and we are able to return to a functional lifestyle sooner.

We can use the understanding we created in Section 12.1, which helped identify how our job affects our health. If the movements we make at work aggravate our pain, then we need to see if we can eliminate them temporarily. If the work environment creates emotional or mental distress, then we may need to work from home or change offices. If the hours we work create too much fatigue, then maybe we need to cut back. In the United States we are taught to prioritize our work over all else and if we can't live up to those standards, then we don't have a job. We are just beginning to learn that healthy people do better work and sometimes that means NOT prioritizing the job when we are unwell.

Asking for what you need can be terrifying. We don't want to admit vulnerability or weakness because we feel that our worth or value within the job will be compromised. We don't want others to perceive us as lazy or unable to carry our weight. We don't want to lose our jobs! But healthy work places create conditions in which people thrive in their physical and mental lives, in part because that's when people contribute the best. Finding roles that work well for each individual in a workplace also helps. Not everyone functions the same and that allows us to balance out one another and come together as a team. If our needs don't match the needs of the company, then it would be better for everyone if we found a better fit.

When I suffered my first back injury, I was working at an outdoor adventure school. I was the Spanish teacher and did that part of my job well. Because of the nature of the school, I was also expected to go on outdoor outings with the students, biking, climbing, and boating. My back injury prevented me from doing these activities and pushing through wasn't even an option. For the rest of the school year, I adapted my duties to encompass classroom teaching and mentoring, but at the end of the year we decided that I needed to find a different job.

That job had provided me much happiness when I was in good health, but it didn't fit once I was injured. It was better for me and the school to find a more suitable match. Trying to push through would have prolonged my injury, and it would have led to frustration within the school when I couldn't contribute equally. **When we admit our needs, we have to be open to the possibility that our current position may not be able to accommodate them. We have to trust that we can either find a**

new role or a different job that will fit our needs better. But the most important thing is to be honest with what we need.

You can practice acknowledging your needs with the following exercise.

12.3 ACKNOWLEDGING OUR NEEDS AT WORK

You can begin with a breathing and centering exercise. Bring your awareness to your body and reconnect with its experience. Scan through your body in non-judgment, listening to how it's doing in this moment. Ask your body what it needs.

What does your body need to heal?

How does this align with the conditions at your workplace?

You can return to Exercise 11.1 and remember how your job affects your well-being.

What needs to change at your work for you to be able to prioritize your health and well-being?

Do you need to change your schedule?

Do you need to change your duties?

Do you need to change your role?

Do you need to change your location?

Allow yourself to acknowledge all of your needs without holding back. If you hear that voice in your head that says, "They won't accept that. That's not possible. I'll lose my job," quiet that voice for now. Right now all you are doing is honestly acknowledging what would support your healing best. Let your mind run free.

Once we know our needs, we have to express them. Yikes! I know how hard this is. I have lost jobs after expressing my needs, but I always found a new job that better supported my health. We change and shift throughout our lives and our needs change with us. Trying to fit into one job forever may not be what's best for our well-being. Expressing our needs honestly gives us the opportunity to evaluate whether the position we are in is a good fit. It also allows our employer to understand us better and help us to decide if the job is best for us.

Openly expressing our needs gets everyone on the same page. If you aren't communicating your needs, yet you grow frustrated with your experience at work, or fall behind, or don't show up, it reflects poorly on you. If you express your needs, you give your employer and coworkers the opportunity to support you by accommodating those needs so that you can continue to contribute. You give both parties the ability to decide the best path forward, and if it means changing jobs, you will probably be better off.

My partner was a project manager who worked on big construction projects. He had to move every few years to be on site for each build. His stress was extremely high, and his lifestyle suffered. He wasn't getting enough sleep, and he didn't have time to exercise or go out with friends. All he did was work and drink. His alcoholism got out of hand and he started falling behind on the job. He would show up late to work or sometimes not at all—yet, trying to keep up with work was what contributed to his inability to get well.

In order to recover, he quit his job and moved to Colorado where he worked at a ski area for one year. The outdoor lifestyle, low-pressure job, and friendships supported his recovery. When he was feeling more stable, he got another job as a project manager. This time he had to fly every other week to his job site. The stress and fatigue built again, but this time he took action sooner. He recognized that this job could not meet his needs for well-being. The long hours, weekly travel schedule, constant hotels, and high-stress environment did not support his health.

He knew that he needed a regular workout routine, positive social interactions, healthy meals, quality sleep, and downtime. This job could not provide him with that lifestyle, so he switched careers. He is now an engineer and works an 8-5 job with half-days on Fridays. His work is not nearly as high pressure, and he can leave it at the office when he comes home for the evening. His pride took a bit of a hit because he saw his previous job as more prestigious, it paid more, and he felt more important. There was gratification in being able to handle that level of intensity. But when he recognized that he had to prioritize his health over his pride, he started living a much happier life.

When we express our needs and discover that our job cannot accommodate them, we may have to change jobs, but this

doesn't make us a failure. It makes us the hero of our own well-being. We are the only ones who can take care of our health, so we have to make the hard choices to do so. Expressing our needs sets us up for success, because when our needs are met, we are better able to serve others.

When expressing our needs, we're not making demands, judging how others are doing things, or condemning our workplace as unhealthy. We are simply stating what we need to be well. Then we can make an informed decision as to whether or not our current work situation will support us. I always got caught trying to change an entire system to make it healthier for me. This put a big burden on my shoulders, and it never really worked. We're not going to change the whole company. We're just going to ask for what we need within our role. If the company can't accommodate it, find a better fit.

It helps to first acknowledge how we want to contribute and how we see our role in the company before expressing what we need to change. Then we focus on ways we could make those changes while still performing our role. For example, at the outdoor school, I acknowledged my role as the Spanish teacher and recognized that I could still do that part of my job well, but because of my back injury, I needed to step away from the outdoor activities. I could continue in the classroom and take on more mentoring roles, but I could not lead outdoor sports with the students. Now our employer can give their thoughts on what our role is and where we are most important in the company. They can suggest how the company could accommodate our needs. Or they could decide that our role has to include the tasks we are unable to do and that it would be best for us to find a new job. That particular school expressed that they needed teachers to take on the extra sports facilitator roles and that it wasn't feasible for them to keep me on only as a classroom teacher. We mutually decided it would be best for me to relocate. Open communication gives each party the opportunity to share their needs and expectations so that a decision can be made that works well for everyone.

You can use the following exercise to practice expressing your needs.

12.4 EXPRESSING YOUR WORK NEEDS

You can begin with a breathing and centering exercise. Use Exercise 12.3 to acknowledge your needs at work. Then ask yourself what you would like to contribute to the company and what roles you are able to perform. Acknowledge the ways that you are still valuable in the job. Then ask yourself what roles you need to change, adapt, or let go to support your health. How could you change them in a way that still allows you to contribute to the job? Express that to your employer.

Then listen to what your employer needs from you and their expectations. Listen to what they are willing to change for you. If that aligns with what you need to support your health, then you can stay in the job. If they can't accommodate what you need in order to be well, then remember that you have decided to prioritize your health above all else, and trust that you will find a more suitable position elsewhere.

When we change our role at work, change our work load, or leave a job, we can feel we are losing our place in the world. We tie so much of our identity and worth to the job that we do that when we can't do that job anymore we feel like we have lost ourselves. It is important to remember that we have worth outside of our work. Thich Nhat Hanh always taught that it doesn't really matter what we do. Whether we are a janitor or the president of the United States, our role isn't who we are. The most important thing is who we are being and what we are cultivating within ourselves that we can share with the world. If we are the president, but we don't live true to our values or create love in the world, then our role means nothing and we make very little positive impact on the world. If we are a janitor, but everyday we give love and spread kindness in the world, then we are having a very large impact. Who we are being and how we are showing up, matters more than which job we are showing up for.

As we adapt our work to accommodate our illness or injury, remember that our worth and value is not tied to our job. Return to the values of the heart and remember that those values can be cultivated and grown, no matter our job. We find a job that supports our well-being so that we can show up for whatever we do as the best version of ourselves. If we are working an important job, but our poor health makes us angry, stressed, and selfish, then we are not serving the world around us. **We need to be healthy in body, mind, and spirit in order to show up well**

for whatever we do. We pick a job that supports our well-being so that we can support the well-being of the world.

My client who quit her job to take care of her health had been doing Bible translation in Africa. The job provided her with a deep sense of value and worth, because she was spreading the word of God, giving remote tribes the possibility of knowing Jesus. When she quit that job, we had to reestablish the source of her real worth. We looked into what it meant to live in the spirit of Jesus. We found that, for her, it was less important to convert others and more important to live in the spirit of Jesus. We saw that the stress of her work in Bible translation was actually making her less able to live the love and compassion of Jesus in her daily life. She was often tired and frustrated in that work, without the ability to be kind to others. When she stopped doing the job associated with her faith, she was better able to live in her faith.

Reestablish what matters most to you. Remember who you want to be out in the world. Remember that it has very little to do with what title you are given. Find a job that allows you to be well so that you can be the person you want to be.

You can use the following exercise to find your value and worth outside of your job.

12.5 FINDING YOUR VALUE AND WORTH OUTSIDE OF YOUR JOB

You can begin with a breathing and centering exercise. Follow your breath back into your heartspace and reconnect with your true essence. Remember what it is that you value most.

Remember what's really most important to you. Remember who you want to be out in the world and how you want to show up for yourself, others, and the world.

Can you stay aligned with this heart center even if you don't have the job you want?

Can you still contribute light and love to the world even if you aren't working?

Can you still live in the spirit of your faith?

Can you still live as your truest self?

Recognize that if your job is not supporting your health and well-being, it becomes difficult for you to stay aligned with the heart. If your job is preventing you from being the person you want to be, then it's time to let it go.

Remember that your greatest worth is in who you are being and that you can only be your best self if you are healthy and balanced in mind, body, and spirit. Find a job that allows you to stay aligned.

13

Obstacles to Listening

As we take these steps towards listening to and honoring our bodies through illness and injury, many obstacles may get in our way. Most of the time these obstacles are fears, fears that tell us it's not safe or acceptable to honor our true needs. These fears keep us from making hard choices that would support our health. They may lie hidden in our subconscious, telling us that we can't do what we need to do in order to heal. They are triggered by a perceived threat to our basic needs: safety, nourishment, love, belonging, and acceptance. They may have formed from past experiences, what our family or society tells us, or our belief systems. No matter their origin, we have to acknowledge them so that we can move through them to the choices that serve us best.

Fear of the healthcare system

Many of us have a fear of the health care system. We don't trust that it truly has our best interest in mind. We fear that it is controlled by money in a bureaucratic system that only supports certain drugs and certain treatments. We also fear that health care professionals make mistakes, misdiagnose, and mistreat our symptoms. This feels like a threat to our basic need of safety and nourishment. Some of these fears are legitimate, and we do need to stay aware and informed when being treated by any doctor or care provider. But we can't let these fears keep us from seeking the help we need.

I know these fears well. I have had several experiences with the health care system that make me doubt its efficacy in healing me. I was misdiagnosed four times when I had schistosomiasis. I once received a spinal injection and ended up in more pain than when I went in. And I watched as the health care system prescribed my grandma fifteen different medications each one to fix a side-effect caused by one of the other drugs. Nonetheless, I have been grateful for our medical system and what it can accomplish. Furthermore, my skepticism and fear of the medical system may partially contribute to it not working at its fullest potential for me.

When we are fearful of something, we shut down and disconnect from it. Then we make assumptions from afar and never fully engage. This creates a lack of understanding and leads to more distrust. We then get information from outside sources that solely confirms our skepticism. We rarely learn the whole truth, because we refuse to go to the source due to our lack of trust in it.

We tend to take stories about the health care system that

others have told us, that we read on the internet, or that we experienced at one facility and project them onto the entire system. We lose faith in the system and stop seeking its care. Then we suffer from a severe injury or illness and return to the system, carrying all of our skepticism with us. We don't communicate well with the doctors and they no longer have all of our medical history. Because they only see one small part of our health, this illness at this time, they provide a limited-scope solution, a pill or procedure to treat this one symptom. Then we lose touch with that doctor; the next time we face a problem, we visit a different doctor, who gives us another quick fix for the new ailment. Maybe all of these quick fixes start interfering with one another and start causing other problems. In this scenario, the medical system is not the sole problem.

In order for the health care system to work well for us, we have to build a relationship of reciprocal understanding and trust. We need open communication and integral care. Doctors can't treat your whole being if they don't know anything about you and, because we no longer build relationships with our doctors, it's hard for them to truly understand us. They have started to treat symptoms because we have asked them to do so. We seek quick fixes and when those don't work or backfire, we blame the doctor. But it's a mutual problem.

When my partner was stuck in addiction, he sought out psychiatrists who would easily prescribe drugs. If a psychiatrist tried to ask him questions or get him to share his emotions, he shut down and moved on. His preferred psychiatrist had him fill out a chart that confirmed he had ADHD and handed him a prescription for Adderall. This is all too common in our health care world and happens with a variety of drugs. I had the same experience when I began counseling. My first stop was a government-sponsored clinic; the therapist asked me a few questions and then asked if I wanted to be prescribed antidepressants or anti-anxiety medication. When I said I didn't want meds, she seemed at a loss. So I sought a different counselor who focused on mindset. When a patient decides to heal, they will seek a doctor who will actually help.

We as patients need to take responsibility for our own health. We need to build a relationship with our doctor and clearly communicate about our definition of health, the kind of care we desire, and the kind of treatments we prefer. The better our own understanding of our health, the better we are able to explain it to our doctor.

Doctors have in-depth knowledge of the body and its ailments, and they know a wide variety of treatments. However, they don't know everything going on within our body, and many of them lack an integral view of health. Specialists focus their knowledge on one area of the body and may lack knowledge about how ailments and treatments in that area will affect the rest of the body. They may not even ask questions about the rest of your body, because they focus on the one area they know best. This is fantastic when you want a surgeon who has done one surgery hundreds of times and is the best in their field, but when that work causes trouble elsewhere, you may need to ask someone else for support.

I experienced this with my ACL reconstruction. My surgeon was great at putting knees back together and my physical therapist was great at following the ACL recovery protocol, but neither considered how this ACL surgery would affect my compromised lumbar spine. Halfway through the physical therapy, I started getting stabbing pain in my hip and down my leg. I told my therapist about it and about my past back injury, and she modified the movements, but urged me to continue so that the knee would recover. The disc ruptured again due to my lopsided movements and I suffered nerve impingement, losing feeling and mobility in my right leg and foot. I had to switch gears from ACL recovery to back recovery and the journey to healing became much longer. I don't blame the doctors or therapists. I should have been more proactive in seeking care that would consider more than just my knee, but it was a wake-up call to always consider the whole body and not merely one part.

Know your doctors and their specializations. Know who to ask which questions and where to turn for integral health. Specialists are necessary for localized issues, but integrative medicine doctors will help you look at the whole picture and make sure you are creating balance and health throughout your body. Understand how doctors of Western medicine are trained. Many are taught to prescribe pharmaceuticals first and trained for specific procedures and treatments. If that's not where you want to start, ask for a different approach or find a different doctor. Doctors are human, too. They will make mistakes. It is helpful to get several opinions and to keep trying until you find a doctor that feels right to you.

Entrusting our lives and health to someone else is scary. If we are ignorant about what our health care providers prescribe us, inject, or do to our bodies during procedures, it can feel like we are blindly handing our lives over to them. We can ease this fear by staying informed and making choices. The decision to have a procedure means we trust the doctor to perform it. But we maintain ownership: we think intentionally and inform ourselves so that we feel confident in our choice.

Don't let fear keep you from using the health care system. It serves a purpose and, when necessary, does its job well. Understand your fears and empower yourself by asking questions, researching, and self-advocating. Make the choices that feel right for you, and then take an active role in your healing.

13.1 TRUSTING THE HEALTH CARE SYSTEM

You can begin with a breathing and centering exercise. Bring your awareness back inward and ask your body and mind how you feel about the health care system, about your doctors, about your care facilities.

Do you trust that they have your best interest in mind?

Do you trust that they are choosing treatments that align with your definition of health and healing?

Do you trust that they are the best source of this care?

Do you trust that they will do their best work for you?

If you find that there is a lack of trust, notice what that does to your well-being when you are seeking care.

Does it close you off and keep you from sharing?

Does it prevent you from listening to their advice and opinions?

Does it keep you from engaging in your treatments?

Does it prevent you from seeking care when you need it?

How is this affecting your health?

Remember what is most important to you: to be healthy, balanced, and well. Remember that the health care system plays an important role in that. Look into the ways that you can ease your fears by informing yourself and empowering yourself to seek the care that's right for you.

What kind of treatment would you prefer?

Who in your area provides that kind of treatment?

What kind of care are you seeking?

Do you need a specialist and what kind of training would they have?

Do you need an integral doctor to take care of your whole being?

What do you need your doctor to know about you?

What questions do you need to ask to feel confident in your decision?

Remember that you are still in charge of your own health. Inform yourself so that you know which doctors will serve you best. Trust that you are choosing the health care that will be best for you.

Fear of money

For many of us our finances keep us from seeking the care we need. I know this fear all too well. As a kid, I never considered the financial consequences of injury. My parents never once mentioned how much my health was costing them, which, I must say, I am grateful for. Our neighbors have a ten year old, and he stopped by my mom's house with his friend to say hello. They were talking about biking and the boy said, "I'm not allowed to do crazy things because my dad says we can't afford to fix my broken limbs." This and my own adult experience with medical expenses made me realize what a huge role finances play on our health care choices.

It is tremendously scary to feel like you can't afford to take care of your health. It is also tremendously scary to think that the care you receive today may create a financial burden on the rest of your life. Both threaten our basic needs of safety and nourishment. It pains me that we have to face these fears in America. I have often lived on a low income and at times not had the best health coverage, or any health insurance at all. The first time I injured my back was one of those times. I waited far too long to go to the doctor because I didn't have the money to pay.

Then, when I did go, it was emergency care, not comprehensive, because I could only afford one visit. Needless to say, the care did not work.

I dealt with the pain until I moved to Switzerland one year later. There, I had access to all the care I needed and it was affordable. I could go to specialists, alternative care providers, and physical therapists at very accessible prices. This is when I got to explore all kinds of healing options and pick the ones that worked best for me. This is where I was able to truly heal.

In the United States, we are forced into certain health care choices based on what's accepted by our insurance policies. Most of us can't afford to go outside of our network to try alternative options. This greatly limits our access to valuable support. We also stop seeking care once our benefits have run out. I had to stop physical therapy when I had reached my maximum of 25 visits. Even though my back injury was a new condition that would have benefited from physical therapy, the insurance company did not approve the extra sessions. I had to wait six months until my plan renewed the following year to get the care I needed. This is detrimental to us as patients, and to our system as a whole. When we can't get comprehensive care, we don't really get well, and we become stuck in the sickness cycle, prisoners of the system. In my opinion, this ends up costing the system more money than actually curing the patients by giving them all the healing options they could need.

Many stories exist of individuals evacuated by helicopter after sustaining acute injuries in the backcountry, only to spend the rest of their lives paying off debts larger than my mortgage. I have also heard of cancer patients who passed away, leaving their families with medical debt to accompany their grief. Health should be a human right, not a reserved privilege for those who can afford it. In the United States, about 23 million people owe medical debt.[7] This number would be higher if everyone engaged in all of the health care that they preferred. The limitations on our budget prevent us from seeking the care we need and prefer.

I prefer to rely mostly on alternative care practices unless I have an acute injury or illness. I find it more beneficial to create balance and harmony in my body before something goes wrong than to treat the symptoms when it does; but our health care and insurance system do not pay for the bodywork, yoga, mindfulness, and integrative health that keep me in harmony. They only pay to treat the symptoms created when my body falls out of alignment. This system discourages people from staying well by only supporting the unwell. We then have to make the choice to pay for our own health maintenance, which is unattainable for many.

There are ways to shift this dynamic. We as consumers can ask for the care that we prefer. We can advocate for the kind of health care we want. We can ask our doctors to prescribe mindfulness rather than medication. We can ask them to treat us with nutrition and lifestyle changes versus procedures, and we can ask them to refer us to coaches and practitioners who can support us in making those shifts. We can tell them that, before jumping to surgery, we would like to try physical therapy and rehabilitation. And we can show them that we are willing to do the work necessary to create harmony within our own systems rather than relying on drugs or procedures to do it for us.

These shifts won't happen over night. In the meantime, we may have to create our own saving accounts for the kind of care we prefer. Health Savings Accounts (HSA) are a great option and often allow you to use that money on alternative treatments of your choice. Collectives and support groups formed around alternative healing may be able to provide recommendations and financial assistance. Many practitioners offer pay scales depending on income, so that they can serve people of varying incomes. When we find ourselves in need of more care than we can afford, we may turn to social media platforms to ask for assistance, churches and religious organizations that provide aid, or community fundraisers. Learn your options and know that you should never compromise your health needs because of financial limitations.

You can use the following exercise to examine and work through your fear of money.

13.2 TRUSTING YOUR RESOURCES TO ACCESS CARE

You can begin with a breathing and centering exercise. Bring your attention inward and ask your mind and body how you feel about the finances related to your health care.

Do you trust that you have the financial means necessary to pursue all of the health care options you would like?

Do you feel burdened by your medical bills?

Do you feel supported by your insurance and government to take care of your health in the ways that you would prefer?

Do you fear that you won't have enough money to meet your basic health needs?

If you find you lack trust that your finances will allow you to pursue the care you need, then observe what effect that has on your health and well-being.

Do you deny yourself the care you need due to your financial limitations?

Do you feel stuck with certain kinds of procedures or treatments because they are covered by your insurance?

Do you not engage in self-care practices that would keep you well because you don't have the financial means?

Does it prevent you from honoring your true needs and preferences around health and healing?

Remember what is most important to you: to be healthy, balanced, and well.

What would you do for your health if money was not a factor?

Remember that there are different options for acquiring the finances necessary to care for your health. Remember that no amount of money is worth the loss of your health. Return to your intentions to prioritize your health and explore financial options that allow you to do so.

Ask for pay scales.

Create an HSA account.

Look into health care-sharing organizations.

Find fundraising support groups.

Sign up for a membership-based health plan.

There are always options that allow you to finance the kind of healthcare that you prefer. Empower yourself by knowing what's most important to you and finding the resources that allow you access to it.

Fear of change and aging

We all have a fear of change. Change means uncertainty and uncertainty feels like a threat to our basic need for safety and belonging. The uncertainty of change keeps us in habits and routines that may not serve us well. We may know that our lifestyle is making us ill, but the idea of altering our lifestyle is too big to fathom. Instead, we ask for pills and surgeries so that we can continue eating what we want and behaving how we want. This will never create sustainable health. Sometimes we have to let go of the familiar to embrace what's best for us.

A fear of change can also lead us to resist aging. We want our bodies to stay the same forever—to look young and beautiful, and be capable of operating at the high pace and intensity of our youthful body. As we notice that our body sags in new places or that we fatigue more quickly, we want try to counteract it. We seek hormone therapies, injections, surgeries, and pills so that our body can ward off the inevitable. But aging is a natural progression of life. Aging allows us to appreciate new activities and prioritize new values. Instead of resisting aging, we should embrace it. We can watch and observe the ways our body is changing and ask ourselves how to make the most of it. Aging is not the end of everything fun; it's an opportunity to discover a whole new meaning of fun.

We often latch onto one way of being in the world. If we're athletes, we push our bodies and seek reward in its performance. If we're fast-paced achievers, we strive for the next level. If we're wanderers, we seek the next big adventure. But what happens when our bodies ask us to slow down? We fear that change will make us lose who we are. In a sense, we are right. A part of us will soften or disappear, but a part of us will also come to life and blossom. Change can uncover our whole selves. It can push us from boxes we have put ourselves in and help us realize that we are more than we thought. We might discover that we were amazing athletes or successful CEOs, *and* that we can be amazing artists, creators, coaches, writers, or philanthropists. **Sometimes we have to let go of who we were to see the full potential of who we can become.**

Embracing uncertainty can be tremendously healing. Uncertainty is the only guarantee in life. Trying to prevent life from changing is like trying to put a breeze into a box. It destroys its true nature so that it can no longer be its true refreshing self. A breeze needs to flow in order to be a breeze, and life needs to change in order to be alive. Sometimes illness and injury force changes on us that we didn't want, but that shouldn't keep us from using them for the greater good. We never know what will manifest because of the changes that illness and injury motivate in our lives. When we embrace the changes they are making in our lives, we see that they can lead to inspiring new places.

When I was going through my back injury, I resisted change with all my might. I thought I knew exactly what made me happy and I was angry at the world for taking it away. I saw only what I was losing. I was losing my job, my sports, my friends, and eventually my home. But those losses ended up leading to positive change in my life. I discovered mindfulness and meditation. I started my own business in a field that I adore. I made a new home in a place that suited me better, and I built new relationships that supported me in who I was becoming. **Change can be scary, but if we lean in and focus on what we want to experience more of in our lives, change can be our biggest support.**

You can use the following exercise to make peace with change.

13.3 MAKING PEACE WITH CHANGE

Begin with a breathing and centering exercise. Bring your attention inward and ask your mind and body how they feel about change.

Is there a change in your life that you are resisting?

Are you seeing only the negative sides of change?

Are you avoiding making changes that would benefit your health?

What are you afraid of losing?

If you are resisting change, then notice what affect that is having on your health and well-being.

Is resisting change keeping you from healing?

Are your old habits creating illness or injury in your body?

Is your body at peace with the choices you are making?

Turn your attention to your heartspace. Remember what the heart values most. Remember that your biggest priority is your health and well-being. Ask the heart how it feels about change.

What would you like to experience more of in your body?

What would you like to experience more of in your mind?

What would your heart like you to be experiencing?

Can you imagine changes in your life that could manifest more of those experiences?

What changes is your body asking you to make to take care of your health and well-being?

What kind of change could bring you closer to who you really want to be and what you want to experience?

Approach change with an open mind and heart. Believe that, although you may be losing some things, you will also gain many more. Trust that this change will bring you closer to who you want to be in the world and what you want to be experiencing. Lean into the change and embrace it.

Fear of losing relationships

Illness and injury inevitably create changes in our lives, and these changes affect our relationships. Many of us fear losing relationships, and this threatens our basic need of love, belonging, and acceptance. We wonder if we will still have a place in our loved ones' lives when our physical abilities are altered. Some of our relationships will fall away, but others will form in their place, and these new relationships will likely align better with the person we are becoming.

As mentioned in Chapter 11, our relationships will adapt with the changes brought by our illness or injury. Instead of fearing these changes and looking only at the potential for loss, we can look at the possibility for growth. True relationships use challenge to understand one another on a deeper level. They lean into difficulty and ask "how can we love each other better through this." Relationships like this cultivate love, belonging, and acceptance. Relationships that can't do this aren't a good resource for meeting our true needs. When we lose these kinds of relationships, we are not losing our ability to be loved and accepted.

When we recognize that we value relationships because they are a source of these basic needs, we can open to the idea of receiving these needs in many different ways, not just from one person. We can remember that our true sense of love, acceptance, and belonging is found within us. It is in our connection to the world and our understanding of our place within it. Relationships can help these feelings develop and grow, but they are not their only source. This recognition eases our fears of change within our relationships. Relationships may come and go, but love, acceptance, and belonging always remain.

When facing the fear that illness and injury may cause us to lose relationships, we can ask ourselves which relationships are able to deepen and grow through the experience and which are not. Both will likely exist in our lives. We can appreciate the relationships we need to release, recognizing the role they played before and realizing they no longer serve as the best sources of connection now. We may grieve their loss, but the grief will lessen when we realize that we have not lost our only sources of love, acceptance, and belonging. We then look to relationships that may deepen through the experience and ask ourselves how we might nourish them. Return to Chapter 10 for that process. We recognize that, though a relationship may shift and change, it doesn't have to end, and these changes elevate it to a new level, one we didn't believe possible.

We can also stay open to new relationships forming. If we focus only on our old relationships and those we are losing, we may miss marvelous opportunities to connect with someone new. As our lives shift and change, new people enter them. We can set intentions about the types of people we would like to meet and align the intentions with the new lifestyle we are choosing to live. These people may be just the friends we need on our new journey.

You can use the following exercise to make peace with the fear of losing relationships.

13.4 MAKING PEACE WITH THE FEAR OF LOSING RELATIONSHIPS

You can begin with a breathing and centering exercise. Bring your attention inward and ask your mind and body if they have a fear of losing relationships.

Are you afraid that this illness or injury will end some of your relationships?

How does that affect your behavior and attitude in those relationships?

Which relationships are you afraid of losing?

What do these relationships provide you that you are most afraid to lose?

Now examine how this fear affects your well-being.

Are you avoiding addressing your health issues for fear of losing relationships?

How does this fear affect your behavior and attitude in those relationships?

How does this fear affect your emotional and physical well-being?

Are you able to engage in the positive sides of the relationship?

Now examine what you value most in relationships and how to nourish that.

What aspect of these relationships are you afraid of losing?

What do you value most in your relationships?

What do they provide to you: is it love, acceptance, and belonging?

Are they your only source of these feelings?

Which relationships could continue to be a source of the feelings even through your illness or injury?

What do you need to do to nourish those relationships?

Which relationships may not be a source of these feelings through your illness or injury?

Could you let them go?

Now open yourself up to developing new relationships.

What type of connections would support you best in your healing process?

What would you like to experience more of in your relationships now?

Where might you find more of these types of connections?

Give your relationships the freedom to change and shift during this process. Remember that love, acceptance, and belonging reside within you. They are energies that are always present in the world and losing one relationship doesn't mean that you lose these feelings. Feel them in your own heart. Feel them for yourself. Receive them from the world around you and trust that when you are living from the heart you will always have love, acceptance, and belonging.

Fear of judgment

Making heavy medical decisions is a daunting task and a fear of judgment only makes the task more difficult. This fear may prevent us from engaging in the healing process that feels right for us. This judgment may come from our doctors, family, friends, or community. Everyone has opinions on healing, and they often share them without invitation. These differing opinions may make us feel like ours is wrong, and we may question our choices. In some cases, people feel strongly and want to push their views on us. We may already feel more delicate and vulnerable when sick or injured, and these pushy opinions can feel like attacks. If we are in a situation in which we fear our love, acceptance, belonging, or safety will be threatened because of a choice we make, we may choose to compromise our own wishes and in turn our health.

Differing opinions are valuable when facing heavy medical decisions. We should inform ourselves of the different options available, but ultimately the decision should remain our own. We must stay aware of the intent behind people's informative support. If they try to convince rather than explain, we may want to seek different sources of information. Most people have biases based on their beliefs and preferences. Hearing other's ideas can open us to new options, but we always should remember that a new idea is just one way of approaching things.

The most difficult place to feel judgment is from our loved ones and family. If they don't agree with our medical choices, we can feel alone and unsupported. Recognizing the source of judgment can help us understand. Our loved ones face many fears of their own when we are sick or injured; in order to pacify those fears, they will do whatever they can to make us better. Sometimes this means that they cling to their beliefs about what we need to heal and try to persuade us to agree.

Their judgment doesn't come from a place of non-acceptance. It comes from a place of love. They fear losing someone they care about. We can try to comfort them by explaining the reasons for the choices we make, but they're really seeking reassurance that we will be alright. So we have compassion for one another and recognize that we are trying to keep our loved ones safe. We try to remember that there is no one right way to heal, and the only right way in a particular situation is the one that feels best for the patient.

We may also feel judgment from our peers and healthcare providers. Everyone has a different idea of health and how to attain it, based on their past experiences, values, and priorities. No one will have the same healing journey. Yet we often want to project our ideas of health and healing onto others. This doesn't come from a place of malice; typically, we are trying to help in the only way we know how. If something worked for us and we strongly believe in it, we will probably try to convince others to do the same. If we are too adamant, this can lead others to feel judged or unheard.

If our peers try to convince us to heal in a way that doesn't feel right for us, we can acknowledge their true intent. Are they trying to harm us and make us feel bad? Or are they motivated by the desire to help? Most likely, they want us to feel better and are stuck in their own mindset regarding how to accomplish that. We can acknowledge the positive sides of their advice and set boundaries when that advice goes too far. It is important to return to our own definition of health, what's most important to us, and how we want to engage in our healing. If we are grounded in those, then what other people say and think won't affect us as much.

As a mindfulness coach, I work alongside other practitioners. I also frequent different practitioners for my back injury. Each has a different perspective on what works. Some friends have told me that if I accept Jesus into my life, my back would be healed. Some friends have told me that my pain is emotional and, in order to heal, I simply need to make peace with emotional baggage. Some tell me my pain is psychosomatic, and I need only tell myself it's not real. Some friends called me crazy for not having surgery and thought that everything would be better if I just got an operation. Some told me to stop doing intense exercise and some told me to continue life as before.

With the many voices giving directions on how to heal, we will never be able to please all of them. No matter what, someone will feel like we're approaching our healing incorrectly and they may judge us for our choices. Ultimately, the choice is ours and our bodies will only heal when we trust the choices we make and fully believe that they will work. We must direct our healing, whether we choose to trust one doctor and his methods completely or choose to create our own assortment of methods. The most important thing is that we believe it's the right healing path for us.

You can practice making peace with your fear of judgment with the following exercise.

13.5 MAKING PEACE WITH THE FEAR OF JUDGMENT

You can begin with a breathing and centering exercise. Bring your attention inward and ask your mind and body if they have a fear of judgment.

Are you afraid that others will judge you for your healing choices?

Do you make choices to please others?

Do you let the judgment of others change the choices you make around healing?

Are you still able to hear your own needs and opinions over the opinions of others?

Now examine how this fear is affecting your health and well-being.

Are you engaging in the healing methods you prefer?

Do you believe fully in the healing choices you are making?

How does this fear affect your relationship with yourself and your trust in yourself?

Does this fear keep you from listening to your own body?

Now return to your definition of what health means. Return to your values and what you want to prioritize in your healing. You can also return to Chapter 1 to review this.

What does health mean to you?

What kind of healing methods feel best for you?

What do you believe would help you heal?

What do you value most and what do you want to prioritize in your healing journey?

Now that you are confident of your own healing truth, you can listen to the opinions and perspectives of others, knowing that they may add value to your own understanding of health. Notice when those opinions start turning to judgment. Observe your limits and set boundaries so that you can honor your own truth. As you are listening to others' opinions on your healing options, notice how they are affecting you.

Are they speaking out of love?

Are they motivated to help you heal?

Are you feeling judged?

Is it hard for you to hear your own needs?

What do you need in order to stay in your own truth right now?

Ask them for what you need in order to hear and honor your own truth around healing. Remember that the only right way to heal is the way that feels right to you.

Patience and time

All of us would love to heal on our desired time frame—and usually that's immediately. Unfortunately, true healing almost always takes time, and it's hard to be patient when we aren't feeling well. Waiting triggers the fear that we will never get well. It also triggers our fear of dying. We fear that we may just keep deteriorating until we pass away. To combat these fears, we do everything within our power to force healing to happen now. This may create even more unrest and panic in us when we see that healing is not happening. We may feel like we are losing control of our own well-being. The expectation that we should heal immediately to avoid suffering only makes us suffer more when we realize we can't.

The need to heal immediately pushes people to make health choices that may not be the most beneficial. These choices may create long-term complications or dangerous side effects, and most of the time they don't actually heal the root cause of the problem. The body wants to heal, but sometimes it needs a grace period in order to do so. Pushing it to heal too quickly may create more damage in other areas or worsen the existing ailment. Time is the secret ingredient to every healing journey. Even in spontaneous healings, people had to be patient with their ailment before that miraculous moment occurred.

Patience brings peace to the healing process. Acknowledging that healing takes time allows us to stop the desperate search to fix it now and engage fully in the step-by-step process of getting well. We do what we need to in each moment to bring our-selves the highest possible level of comfort and well-being in our particular state. Instead of racing in a panic towards the finish line in order to feel peace, we nurture ourselves and find peace here and now. We constantly ask ourselves, "what do I need in order to be at peace in this moment with this experience?" and we take the next step to attain it.

I think of patience as the ability to be intentionally present in our experience. Impatience is the refusal to accept our current experience. We want to rush out of it into the next one. We become frustrated, closed, and angry in the present, refusing to live with what is and expectantly awaiting what will be. But, as we know, our future is built on each and every present moment, so, if we are living with impatience now, we are not building a peaceful future. Patience means loving and accepting what's in the here and now. It's using each precious moment we're given to cultivate more of what we want to experience in life. If our expectations aren't being met, then we loosen our grasp on them and look around to find the positivity we can engage with now. Each moment is a gift; so don't waste it waiting for something better to arrive.

When we are sick or injured, the last thing we want to do is be patient. We feel like we are living the worst moments right now, and we just want to arrive at feeling better. We don't want to be in this experience. Resistance to the present only makes our suffering stronger, and it doesn't help us heal. We can engage with intention and growth even in the hardest of times. These hard times are often when we learn the most about ourselves and experience the most profound transformations. If we close our eyes and bear down until things change, we won't receive the deep teachings. This too belongs. This too is a part of our journey, and we have to walk through it in presence to experience true healing. Patience is being with each moment, even the ones filled with suffering, and using that moment to generate more of the wisdom, understanding, and light that will support a beautiful future.

We will come in and out of our ability to do this. At some moments, I give in to the anger and frustration, and I curse this present moment and will the next one to arrive, hoping it will bring less pain. But I recognize that this only makes me suffer more. I see that it builds walls within me that stop the healing flow of energy. So I let go and accept. This is where I am right now. Right now I am experiencing pain and I have a choice. I choose to be with the experience and build the skills that support my well-being through it, and I know that that is what makes me stronger and wiser.

Patience is the ability to be vulnerable and uncertain. It's the ability to sit with the discomfort and pain without fear and anger. It's the ability to trust that you're exactly where you need to be, experiencing exactly what you need to experience. **And it's the ability to surrender to those great unknown powers that give us the exact journey we need in order to grow into the people we are meant to be.**

You can use the following exercise to develop patience.

13.6 CULTIVATING PATIENCE

You can begin with a breathing and centering exercise. Bring your attention inward and ask your mind and body if you are feeling impatient.

Are you willing this experience to end?

Are you closing off and baring down until something changes?

Are you feeling angry and resistant to this present moment, waiting for your expectations to be met?

Now notice what this impatience is doing to your health and well-being.

Are you feeling at peace in your body and mind?

Are you able to relax and let go of tension?

Can you feel a steady continuous flow of energy through you?

Is this helping you to heal?

Now recognize where this impatience is coming from.

Are you afraid of vulnerability?

Are you afraid of discomfort?

Are you afraid of pain?

Are you afraid of uncertainty?

Show yourself compassion for these fears. Recognize that it is hard to be present for pain and suffering. It is hard to be patient through illness and injury. Remind yourself of your intentions.

What do you value most?

What's most important to you?

Who do you want to be out in the world?

How do you want to show up for yourself, others, and the world?

Does your impatience help you to use this present experience to live your intentions?

How could you be present for this experience even if it means suffering in a way that helps you cultivate your true values and grow into the person you want to be?

Trust that this is an equal part of your journey, and it too can serve to generate more compassion, understanding, wisdom, and light in the world. Choose to engage with this experience intentionally, and use it to become the person you really want to be in the world.

4

My Personal Healing Journey

14

My Journey with Pain

Though we all have unique journeys with healing, other people's stories can help us gain more resources for our own journeys and feel a little less lonely along the way. This recount of my healing journey includes difficult and sensitive moments in my family. The stories are told from my perspective and only include what happened to me. They are a one-sided perspective and focus on the traumas that caused my wounding. There were of course many other positive memories that aren't shared here and overall I feel as though I had a very fortunate upbringing. Each member of my family is on their own journey towards healing containing many growth opportunities that they will face in their own way at their own time. None of them should be judged for the stories I share here.

My journey began early on in life. My body was always a reflection of my emotional and mental world. When I was in middle school, I would get horrible stomachaches and headaches that would bring me home from school, a lonely place of fear and anxiety for me. I never felt like I belonged in public school and couldn't navigate the social dynamics of the other kids. I always felt I was under their watchful eye, judged for being myself. I was a perfectionist and put a lot of pressure on myself in sports and academics, and the stress took its toll.

At age 13, I was diagnosed with a rapidly growing tumor in my nasal canal. I had eight different surgeries to remove all of the tumor and then rebuild my jaw and teeth. I had to wear a retainer with fake teeth, and I still remember the embarrassment I felt when removing it to eat my lunch, revealing a gaping hole in my mouth. One day I threw my teeth away along with my leftover food and had to spend the next period digging through the trash with the lunch lady. These times were not all bad. While recovering from each surgery, I got to stay home from school, watch sappy movies, and eat nothing but soup and ice cream. It was the one time I got to let my guard down and be vulnerable. I played the role of peacekeeper and tension-easer in my family, so recovering from surgery felt like permission to be taken care of. It was the only time I felt safe from the pressures of perfectionism.

In high school, I learned to use sports as an easy way to avoid emotions and satisfy my perfectionism. The harder I pushed in sports, the less I had to think about the other stressors of life. Sports also gave me a sense of belonging and acceptance. My body paid the price. My competitive mountain biking took me to the hospital many times, and after one highly traumatic crash, in which I dragged myself two miles up a trail with a fractured femur, I took a break. But I directed my energy into new pursuits, traveling to Ghana to teach English.

Swimming in a freshwater pond gave me schistosomiasis, a rare parasite that lives in your lungs and spreads eggs through your vascular system. The egg accumulation in the capillaries impinges oxygen exchange and can slowly shut down your organs. At the time, I was going to school in Oregon and was facing the usual stresses of beginning college. The rainy gray weather didn't help. When I started to feel fatigue and headaches, I figured it was the season and stress. When I found blood in my stool, I knew something else was wrong. Climbing stairs started to feel like climbing Mt. Everest as my lungs struggled and weakened. I had to drop out of school to return home to Colorado for medical testing. This was the first time I started to lose faith in the medical system.

I knew that my body was facing something much more severe than college stress, but as the doctors failed to find the source, they put the blame back on me. They asked me if I was putting foreign objects up my rectum to cause the bleeding. They tried to push anti-depressants on me. Every week I was poked, prodded, and interrogated by a new doctor. I went to the infectious disease doctor and the gastroenterologist. I had to go through two different colonoscopies before medical staff finally conducted the lab testing the same day the sample was taken (this is crucial with schistosomiasis because the parasite will die in transit and won't be seen). The lab tech happened to be doing his masters thesis on schistosomiasis and was thrilled to see his first live specimen in my intestine lining. This showed me how much of our medical system is left to chance and luck and how many unknowns still exist. It showed me the importance of listening to our own bodies and continuing to question and search until we arrive at a solution that feels good.

These six months of being stuck at home while all of my friends were enjoying their second year of college were a challenge, but I also felt a sense of relief. I wasn't happy at school in Oregon. I missed the sunshine and the mountains. While recovering, I spent a lot of time in the forest behind our house, reconnecting with nature. I rediscovered my passion for painting and spent hours a day creating. Once again, I gave myself permission not to be perfect and not to perform because my body wouldn't let me, and a part of me liked it.

After recovery, I started school in Durango, Colorado, and spent more time skiing and biking than studying. I smoked a lot of marijuana and gave myself permission to just be me. I switched my major to French and leaned into the things that came more naturally to me. After graduating, I moved to France to teach English, and I was healthy and happy.

When I returned home, I felt like I had nowhere to go, like there was no place for me in the United States. I tried to return to my boyfriend in Durango, but that no longer fit. I tried to go home to my parents, but my dad had left my mom and she was struggling with alcoholism, leaving me once again to play the role of tension-easer. I couldn't get out of the states fast enough, so I signed up to teach English in Santiago, Chile. Traveling had always been my way to escape the life I had at home. It was a chance to reinvent myself and leave behind the hurt. But this time I carried my hurt with me.

I couldn't shake the feeling of being unsupported and

vulnerable. I made very little money teaching in Chile and live on the pull-out couch of a one-room apartment that I shared with a Colombian. I never felt I had enough money to buy what I needed or do what I wanted. The city of Santiago was cold in the winter. There was no centralized heating in the buildings so I taught in my down parka. Though we had portable gas stoves to heat the apartment, we had to sit right next to them to feel the benefit. The inversion effect, along with the fishbowl of surrounding mountains, created an air trap for the city's pollution, leaving a black film over everything, including my lungs. I got a chest cold that I couldn't get rid of which eventually turned into pneumonia. After six months, I had to go home. But I didn't know where home was.

When I arrived back at my parent's house in Colorado, my luggage never made it in the door. My dad had returned to my mom, and he wouldn't let me stay at the house because I had taken my mother's side during their separation. I took all of my belongings, which fit into two suitcases, and went to live in my brother's closet in Buena Vista. I slept on a camping pad in a space no wider than my arm span for a month and washed dishes at a local Thai restaurant. When I had enough money saved, I moved into a trailer with a gal fresh out of rehab. I worked my way up from dishwasher to breakfast chef to baker and then got a job teaching Spanish at a local school.

While I was piecing my life back together, my brother's was falling apart. He was drinking heavily and using drugs, which led to unpredictable outbursts and the perception that the world was out to get him, including me. Our last encounter was at a concert held at a local bar. I attended with a date, and my brother showed up halfway through, stumbling and slurring. He headed straight towards my date and shoved him hard, yelling, "Are you fucking my sister! Huh, you little shit? Are you fucking my sister!" He shoved him again before I stepped between the two, averting my brother's anger. He was kicked out of the bar, and I had a panic attack on the front step. In denial of how much my lack of family support affected my over all well-being, I forged ahead, mountain biking my way back to sanity.

I crashed hard, crushing my hip into a pointed rock and was bedridden for a week. I went to urgent care for x-rays but they didn't see anything broken. This mended, but a pain lingered in my lower back and hip. Midway through ski season, I dropped down into a telemark turn on a mogul run and couldn't stand back up. The pain in my low back and down my left leg was so intense that any movement made my body seize. I inched my way back to the car and drove myself home, hoping the pain would go away by morning. It did not.

The pain continued through the following weeks. I didn't have health insurance at the time, so I didn't want to go to a doctor. I couldn't sit, bend forward, twist, or extend my left leg. There was no position that relieved the pain. I slept on the ground because I could find no relief on the soft mattress. I wasn't sleeping. I couldn't do any of the sports that kept me mentally and emotionally well. I struggled my way through teaching, because I couldn't afford to miss work. I would eat standing up. I was, without a doubt, completely falling apart.

Two months later, I was in the same amount of pain, pushing my way through life, when my mom contacted me for the first time in a year to tell me that she and my dad were moving to the

Congo. She said that we needed to meet so that she could give me my birth certificate and other important documents stored at their house. My friend drove me the two hours from Buena Vista to Woodland Park to meet her. We sat across from each other at the donut shop where our family used to stop on our way to cut a Christmas tree. She slid a manila envelope of my life's documents over to me and held my hand, tears streaming down her face. To me, at that moment, it felt like my dad had won. He had successfully stolen her away from me, cutting me out of their lives to punish me for taking her side when he left. I felt I was losing all the support I had in the world. I had lost my brother months before and now I was losing my parents.

Many people link low back pain to the fear of not having enough support in life. I was scraping by on a part-time teaching wage, with no health insurance, a debilitating back injury, and no family around to help me. Friends are amazing, but the basic needs of survival feel like too big of a burden to put on any-one other than blood relatives. So I continued pushing, holding everything within me tightly to prevent it from exploding into a million unrecoverable pieces, and it hurt like hell.

The next year, I got a job at the public middle school and obtained health insurance. I immediately made an appointment with the spine center of Denver. I drove myself the three hours to get there, and by the time I arrived, I could barely stand. Every step sent knives stabbing down my leg. The doctor did an MRI, diagnosed it as a ruptured disc, and gave me a spinal injection that same day. He stabbed a giant needle into my spine and then sent me on my way to drive myself home.

Ten miles from the clinic, I had to pull off the highway and call an old friend to pick me and my car up. The pain was so bad that I couldn't push the gas or brake. My friend came to get me and her brother drove my car back to her apartment. The next morning, I went to move my car and found the ignition torn apart, wires dangling from the gaping hole. Someone had tried to steal my car, but luckily, the gas pump had been going out so they couldn't hot-wire it to get away. I got the car towed to a mechanic and ended up at my friend's parents' house, cared for by her loving mother. But this was like a band-aid on an exploded limb. There was no amount of care from a friend's mother that could fill this pit of fear, loneliness, and self-pity within me.

I stayed in Buena Vista for one more year, stuck in a state of depression. Western medicine wasn't working for me, but I didn't know where else to turn for help. We all like to believe that, if and when our bodies fail, all we will have to do is spend some time on meds or in a hospital and then everything will be OK. Nothing can prepare you for when this lie crashes down around you and you realize you are alone with your pain, and no one can help.

Every time my friends went out to ski, I felt betrayed and abandoned. When they returned, bragging about their epic ski runs, anger boiled in me burning my insides and isolating me from the relationships. My pain stole the fun in my life. No matter what I was doing or where I was, a little piece of my attention was always glued to the agony within my body, detracting from my present experience. I wasn't able to perform in my job, which included going on outdoor adventures with my students. I wasn't able to engage in relationships. I couldn't enjoy my favorite hobbies. The pain had taken over my existence. I believed that if I wasn't able to live life like before the injury that it wasn't worth living at all.

My dear friend and acupuncturist did her best to help me heal. She peeled me off the couch and took me to the edge of the mountains where we walked on a flat gravel road through the forest. She reminded me that the beauty of nature was still available, even if I couldn't fly through it on skis. We picked apples, cooked good food, and watched movies together. She gave me acupuncture treatments on the floor of our rented house. But the depression remained. I knew it was time for a dramatic change.

The path towards true healing

True healing takes time because it's a total transformation—from the inside out. It begins with the recognition that what you've been doing in the past isn't serving you now and you develop a deep desire to change. It's an intention to heal built from the understanding that you have to do so in order to survive. I knew that I couldn't continue life in the same way. I was stuck in my suffering because I thought the only way to heal was to go back to the way I was before the injury. But who I was before the injury wasn't serving me well. If I had gone back to living in that way, my body would simply continue to break down. In order to heal, I had to let go. Let go of who I was before so that I could become the person I was meant to be now.

I started by moving to Geneva, Switzerland. A change in geography isn't necessary for a change in self, but when you find yourself as stuck as I was, it can be the crowbar that wrenches you from the ditch. Europe was always my refuge. It's where

I went to find myself starting at age 16, when I participated in an exchange year to Switzerland. It was here that I found an identity apart from my family. There was something safe and nurturing about Europe for me. Everything felt stable; the systems worked, the communities were strong, and the medical system was accessible. Life felt softer there, less aggressive, less individualistic, and less pressured. My lack of family also felt more acceptable since I was halfway around the world. People took me in, and I ended up with several adopted family systems. It was my sanctuary.

When healing, it is important to create a safe space for yourself, whether you create it within or find it in the world around you by going somewhere comforting. My safe space was graduate school in Geneva. Within this safe space, I was able to explore more healing options. The medical system in Switzerland allowed me to see all kinds of alternative healers. I saw osteopaths, body workers, physical therapists, and reflexologists. Eventually, an energy worker told me that my body wasn't ready to heal and needed more time.

At first, this was hard for me to understand. Of course my body wanted to heal! Why would a body want to stay in pain? But, after I started my research into mindfulness and meditation, I began to understand. It didn't want me to go back to the way I was before, and until I shifted my perspective it was going to continue giving me problems. My perspective of myself and life was creating the behaviors and habits that were destructive to my physical well-being.

The shift happened slowly. Every Friday I would take the funicular up Mt. Saleve on the outskirts of Geneva. I would walk twenty minutes up the forest path to the Shedrub Choekher Ling Monastery, and I would sit in the meditation and philosophy classes for two hours. At first it was torture. The silence seemed to provoke all the antagonizing thoughts within me. My body wanted to move. It told me I wasn't being productive, this was a waste of time, there were so many things to figure out and get done and this was getting in the way. But in the philosophy classes, I felt I was hearing my own truth spoken back to me after having forgotten it long ago. The monastics were teaching me the impermanent nature of all things, the truth of suffering, the nature of emotions, and my own ability to shift my reality. Everything I was hearing made sense, and each word brought lightness to my life.

I decided to do my master's research on the use of meditation and mindfulness in language acquisition and spent the next two years in Geneva studying the art of being mindful. I went to retreats and workshops through Thich Nhat Hanh's Plum Village tradition, and each one helped me to uncover more about my own mind and how it was forming my reality. I noticed all of the thought patterns and beliefs that were keeping me stuck in my pain. There were a lot.

I recognized how much of my identity was linked to my performance in sports, in work, in life. I thought my worth was measured by what I could do and produce rather than by who I could be. I believed that people would only value me if I could keep up with them on the ski slopes and outdo them in work and life. My perspective was that if I needed help or couldn't sustain perfection, then I would be a burden to others and unworthy of their love. Safety was linked to my ability to be perfect. If I was perfect, I was safe. Yet it was this need for perfection that was breaking me.

During a ten-day silent meditation retreat, I had the revelation that the only way to heal was to develop a forgiving and compassionate relationship with myself. No one else was responsible for my pain. I was the one who had to shift my perspectives on life and learn how to be happy in spite of my body's limitations. I had to see that there was value to me and to life even if I couldn't be the best at sports or work or life. I had to make peace with my pain.

Slowly I began to find things to like about myself and my life that weren't performance related. I started to enjoy my slow walks next to the lake and in the botanical gardens. Gentle yoga and silent meditation started to become as much of a treat as skiing a double black diamond. I spent more time painting and writing, appreciating the simple act of creating. As I slowed down, I became more present for the people in my life and could enjoy time with them, even if we were just having gelato instead of climbing a peak. My connections started to deepen and strengthen because I was prioritizing being with others rather than doing things with others. I realized how wrong I had been before. The more we focus on performing, the less we focus on connecting and the weaker our relationships become. Love doesn't develop from perfection, it develops from true presence, and it's much easier to be present for someone if we aren't focused on beating them.

The same rang true for my relationship with myself and my body. I was recognizing that I could love myself better if I wasn't focused on performing and being perfect. I could love myself better if I was accepting who I was, being gentle with myself, and nurturing myself into a state of well-being. When I was well and balanced, I could be my authentic self in the world and that person was easy to love. My worth had nothing to do with perfection. It had to do with me showing up as my most authentic and heart-centered self.

With these shifts in perspective, my body began to heal. The pain was decreasing and mobility was returning. I was able to ski and bike lightly as long as I stayed aware of my fatigue level and stopped before the pain started. It felt wonderful to go out for a ski and focus more on the experience of being in nature and in the company of friends rather than on my performance. This was true happiness. The ability to be fully present for the experience in front of me without trying to force it to be something better or different. I developed the ability to listen to my body and honor its needs without feeling pressured to keep going or push harder. And I was happy with who I was, even if I was no longer the fastest on the mountain.

These new perspectives were bringing healing into every area of my life. All the tension of perfection and the fear of not being safe was disappearing. I was creating genuine connections that weren't competitive. I didn't feel like I had to perform in order to be loved. I could let my truth and vulnerabilities show and still feel accepted. It was time to take these new lessons home.

The return

The true test of transformation is if we can bring it back to where we were before. We all face this when we return to our parents' house after becoming adults. All of those wonderful steps we took to becoming grounded and solid in who we are fly out the window the second our parents trigger old patterns. The same was true for me. As soon as I moved out of the tree house I was living in and accepted my dad's help to buy my first home, things began to shift. I once again felt under his control, like I had to lose my own voice and truth in order to appease him. I constantly worried that if I didn't attain his approval he would punish me with abandonment, deprivation, or condemnation. My deeper truths were still there, and I could still access them when I took the time to pause and nurture, but the nagging feeling that I wasn't enough was creeping back in.

Starting my own business was one of the biggest challenges of my life. The amount of fear, vulnerability, and self-doubt associated with it is incomparable to anything else. I also began a relationship with a man who loved pushing hard in outdoor sports. This is equivalent to a recovering alcoholic starting a relationship with someone who drinks. It became hard to listen to my body when the person I love and want to spend time with only wants to ski as fast and as hard as he possibly can at all times. It was nothing he was saying to me or doing to me that took me back to that place where I had to perform to be loved. I took myself there. I did it with my business and my sports, and suddenly I had taken on way more than I could handle.

I thought the only way to legitimize my business was to push as hard as I possibly could to be an instant success. I felt like a failure every time a class didn't fill or I didn't increase my profit for a month. My business as a mindfulness coach was becoming very unmindful. I took these same pressures to perform into sports. Because my back had been feeling better, I began to push it harder to keep up with my boyfriend. I would go past the point of fatigue and my back hurt for days afterwards. I thought that he wouldn't want to go with me if he had to wait, or if I had to stop early, and I thought he wouldn't be attracted to me if I wasn't performing well in everything that I did. The perfectionism crept back in. I felt like I had to prove my worth to be loved. I proved my worth by being a champion athlete and a super boss business owner.

If I wasn't performing well, I thought everything I was doing in life and everything I cared about would be discredited and taken away. The pressure to keep up was once again breaking me. Then, on my first ski run one morning, I dropped into some powder-filled trees, one of my skis stuck on a tree, and my body kept going. I heard the pop and felt the rush of pain, but denied the reality. I skied out and learned a week later that I had torn my ACL and the journey to recovery began again.

I pushed my way through surgery and physical therapy accepting help but gritting my teeth until I could get back to self-reliance. The fear that I would lose clients and my business while in recovery lingered. We were building a new studio at the time, and I was laying flooring and painting walls before I could even do a full squat. The pain in my back was building. It prevented me from doing my physical therapy, but I ignored it. After a long day of climbing up and down ladders, I couldn't get off the floor.

The pain was more severe than during the initial injury ten years before. I couldn't stand for more than five minutes without my body shaking in objection. I couldn't put any weight on my right leg without crying. The burning pain traveled down my leg, concentrating in a fireball at my foot as if someone was branding me with a hot iron while simultaneously crushing my foot with an anvil. The only thing I could do was lay on my stomach with a pillow under my chest. I couldn't sleep. The pain would wake me up through the night and I would try to walk it off but would end up back on the floor sobbing. I thought about ending my life several times in those few days. I thought there was no way I could live like this, and I still suffered the illusion that nobody could do anything for me.

My boyfriend forced me to go to the hospital, and I received steroids and pain killers. An MRI showed a ruptured disc occupied most of the space in my spinal canal, crushing the nerve root. They sent me to a neuorsurgeon who told me that surgery wasn't proven to help any more than time. So I went home, using steroids to stop the pain. The progress I had made in Geneva flew out the window. I was back to being a cripple who couldn't do any of her favorite activities. I felt useless, scared, and unlovable.

But this time I was equipped with my mindfulness practice, and I was able to see the patterns emerging. I remembered my supports and returned to the gentler hobbies that still brought me joy. I reached out to my supports and began my body-work and physical therapy. I signed up for meditation retreats and increased my own practice. I watched for the thoughts that weren't serving me, and I used my understanding to shift them.

This was a wonderful opportunity to communicate with my boyfriend about my fears. A relationship built upon perfor-mance will not withstand the ups and downs of life. I told him that I was worried he wouldn't want me anymore if I couldn't do all of the sports that we did together. I shared my insecurities around not being able to keep up. I shared that I felt like a burden when I needed him to support me through my recovery. I shared how important my work as a mindfulness coach was to me and that I needed his support to make it through the developmental stages. **What we discovered together is that the value of partnership doesn't come from what each person is able to do. It comes from how each person is able to love.**

Even though my body was struggling, I could still be present for him in the way I listened, honored his needs, laughed, played, and encouraged. I didn't have to be skiing down a mountain or be a super boss to be worth something to him. True presence is the most valuable asset in a relationship.

Within my work, I cut back on many of my extra projects. I reminded myself of my worth and that the most valuable thing I could do for my business was to stay well. I set boundaries with clients and partners, and I asked for what I really needed. As soon as I did, everything became lighter. I started to enjoy my work again, and it felt sustainable. There was no need to be a slave to the job in order to succeed.

Making peace with western medicine

My new challenge was listening to my own body when it asked me to get surgery. My resistance to Western medicine was still strong. I didn't trust traditional doctors. They didn't look at the whole person, and I knew a problem couldn't be solved without addressing each component: mind, body, and spirit. Everyone told me something different about surgery. The neuorsurgeons themselves said that it wasn't a reliable fix. Some alternative practitioners fed me stories of failed surgeries and how the body needed to and would heal itself. My mom was against surgery, reminding me that the best way to heal was to change my lifestyle and be gentler on my body. A part of me still believed I should be able to heal myself, and a piece of my ego was wounded, accepting the fact that I couldn't. I had tried for ten years to do everything in my power to heal; this time my body was telling me I needed more support.

I had shifted my lifestyle as much as I could, and the pain was still unbearable in simple day to day tasks. The pain created so much tension and fatigue in me that the most gentle routine drained me and filled me with dread. I had to work hard to tune everybody out and listen to my own wisdom. What did I really need?

People started showing up in my life who had had spine surgery themselves or knew of someone who had, so I interviewed all of them. I asked them about their journey up to the surgery, how they chose a surgeon, what experience they had in surgery, and what the recovery was like. Everyone I talked to said that they were glad they had done it and experienced profound relief. I then began to research surgeons. I knew that I wanted a noninvasive surgery. The surgeon I found specialized in arthroscopic spine surgery, which I sought, so I booked the appointment.

I only saw the surgeon for about five minutes during our consultation. He looked over the information his assistant had provided on me and gave his concise opinion: I needed surgery. It was hard to hand my health over to someone I only saw for five minutes, but I kept telling myself that it wasn't about the person, it was about the procedure. He was best at performing the one my body was asking for. I had to trust his skill set, not his persona.

A month before the surgery, I started having dreams about waking up from surgery and not being able to feel my legs. I was terrified of going under anesthesia and worried about its effects on my body. I spent a lot of time in meditation. Reminding myself that I was doing this to support my body and give it relief. Reminding my body that this would help it to live a happier fuller life. I would envision the surgery going well and my body healing quickly. In my many pre-surgery examinations, the medical staff would poke me with needles five times to find a vein, and I had to remind myself that this pain was meant to help, not to harm. I encouraged my body, and this time it felt like it was ready to receive surgical intervention.

Nothing is scarier than putting your mind and body to sleep while someone else cuts into your spine, with no guarantee on how or if you will wake up. But I was ready to trust that this was the best option for my recovery. As the anesthesia kicked in and the sounds of the doctors' voices, country music, and machine beeps faded into the dark abyss, I carried one thought in my mind and heart, this was going to heal me.

Recovery

The pain from surgery was nothing compared to the nerve pain from the injury. The muscles in my leg immediately started to fire again despite their weakness. The feeling in my foot slowly returned. My recovery was quick. Within six weeks, I was hiking and strength training, and in my eighth week, I went on a backpack trip and began mountain biking again. I still had muscle tightness in my back and some imbalances, but full recovery felt attainable with the nerve pain gone.

Thich Nhat Hanh often used the example of a toothache saying that we never appreciate our healthy teeth and how they help us chew until we have an ache. We complain and suffer through the toothache until it is better; then, when it is, we appreciate the tooth for about two days before we forget and once again take that tooth for granted. I experienced immense joy in being able to do my favorite activities and move without pain and its layers of burden and fatigue. My hope is that, after ten years of pain, I will always find simple happiness in my body's ability to move. I am grateful to be able to do my favorite sports again and take a much gentler approach now.

This experience also helped me heal my relationship with conventional medicine. We all need each other. Although there are many problems with our healthcare system, it still serves an important purpose. One doctor will not take care of our whole being, but they will do their part in the bigger picture. It is up to us to stay aware of our needs in mind, body, and spirit and seek out the help that each one requires. It takes a team of varying practitioners and a lot of dedication to truly heal.

Healing Practices and Resources

Everyone's healing journey will look and feel different. The healing modalities and approaches that one person uses may not be effective for someone else. We also all require a different balance of approaches, some using more traditional routes and others using more alternative. There is no right answer. That is why we need access to a wide range of options. Each of us can educate ourselves by researching, asking questions, and trying new modalities. While doing so, we have to remain aware of both how they serve us and their effectiveness. Only you can discern the benefits of something for your health. If it doesn't feel right, don't do it.

I started a non-profit in Montrose, Colorado, to create a collaborative culture around healing. It is called the Healing Collective of Western Colorado. We are open to any local practitioner who wants to work together to learn about one another's practice, support each other's work, cross-refer clients, and work together to help heal the community. We educate the community on their healing and care options and help them to form a support team of practitioners. More of these types of collaborative groups are emerging around the world, and this is the kind of healing spirit you should look for when struggling with illness and pain. You want practitioners who are humble enough to realize they can't do everything on their own and who are informed in other options available for support in mind, body, and spirit.

You can find out more about our collective at healingcollectiveco.com. The following are just a few of your many options for healing. I encourage you to research each one on your own and explore the different options in your area to create your holistic healing team.

Biologically Based Practices

- Hormone Therapy
- Gene Therapy
- Herbal Medicine & Teas
- Dietician & Nutritional Coaching
- CBD & Other Supplements
- Bee Venom Therapy

Body Work Practices

- Physical Therapy
- Chiropractic
- Pilates
- Cranial-Sacral Therapy
- Cupping
- Fitness Coaching

- Foot Zoning
- Reflexology
- Lymphatic Drainage
- Needling
- Visceral Manipulation
- Ionic Foot Bath

Energy Medicine

- Reiki
- Sound Therapy
- Crystals
- Light Therapy
- Access Consciousness
- Shamanism
- Access Bars
- Electromagnetic Fields
- Tapping

Whole Medical Systems Therapy

- Naturopathy
- Nutritional Coaching
- Ayurvedic Medicine
- Acupuncture
- Chinese Medicine
- Homeopathy
- Holistic Medicine

Mind-Body Medicine

- Mindfulness
- Meditation
- Yoga
- Wellness/Life Coaching
- Sound Therapy
- EMDR
- Nature Therapy
- Counseling
- Psychotherapy
- Hypnotherapy

Resources

1.) Albom, M. (2017). Tuesdays With Morrie. Sphere.

2.) Brown, Brene. (2012). *The Power of Vulnerability: Teachings of Authenticity, Connection, and Courage.* Sounds True

3.) Doidge, Norman. (2007). *The Brain That Changes Itself: Stories of Personal Triumph From the Frontiers of Brain Science.* Penguin Life.

4.) Frankl, Viktor E. (Viktor Emil), 1905-1997, author. (1962). *Man's search for meaning : an introduction to logotherapy.* Boston :Beacon Press,

5.) Hanh, Thich Nhat, Berrigan, Daniel. (2001). *The Raft is not the Shore: Conversations toward a Buddhist/Christian Awareness.* Orbis Press.

6.) Hanh, Thich Nhat. (2006). *True Love: A Practice for Awakening the Heart.* Shambhala.

7.) Health Care System Tracker. *The Burden of Medical Debt in the United States, https://www.healthsystemtracker.org/brief/the-burden-of-medical-debt-in-the-united-states, March 10, 2022*

8.) Nepo, Mark. (2013). *Seven Thousand ways to listen,* Atria Books.